GETTING IT RIGHT

Avoiding the High Cost of Wrong Decisions

Deborah C. Sawyer

S^t_L

St. Lucie Press
Boca Raton   London
New York   Washington, D.C.

Figures 4.1 and 4.4   ©Information Plus

Figure 4.2 ©Seena Sharp — Sharp Information Research, 1122 10th Street, Hermosa Beach, CA 90254, Tel.: 310/379-5179, Fax: 310/379-1030, E-mail: ssharp @sharpinfo.com

Figure 4.3 From Fuld, L., *Competitor Intelligence,*© 199X. Reprinted with permission of John Wiley & Sons, Inc. — Fuld & Co., The Fuld & Company Building 126 Charles Street, Suite 2, Cambridge, MA 02141-2130, Tel.: 617/492-5900, Fax: 617/492-7108; E-mail: Info@fuld.com. Web: http://fuld.com

Figure 4.5 Courtesy of Myles P. Kelly — The Marketing Audit, Inc., 1524 Pine Street, Philadelphia, PA 19102, Tel.: 215/545-6620; Fax: 215/545-0888, E-mail: mkelly@worldlynx.net

---

Library of Congress Cataloging-in-Publication Data

Sawyer, Deborah C.
   Getting it right: avoiding the high cost of wrong decisions / Deborah C. Sawyer
      p.   cm.
   Includes bibliographical references and index.
   ISBN 1-57444-228-7
   1. Decision making.   2. Industrial management—Decision making.
 3. Leadership.   4. Strategic planning.
 I. Title.
 HD30.23.S29 1998
 658.4'03—dc 21
 for Library of Congress

                                     98-41575
                                        CIP

© 1999 by Deborah C. Sawyer
St. Lucie Press is an imprint of CRC Press LLC

No claim to original U.S. Government works
International Standard Book Number 1-57444-228-7
Library of Congress Card Number   98-41575?
Printed in the United States of America   1 2 3 4 5 6 7 8 9 0
Printed on acid-free paper

Dedication

This book is dedicated
to all the people
who have ever come through for me.

Contents

Preface

While the actual task of writing this book was measured in months, its preparation was twenty years in the making. For that is when my first company, Information Plus, was established and that is how long I have been working with businesses in North America, as well as overseas, providing support for decision making.

For those readers who might wonder how I came to write a book about decision-making and what makes me think I have the expertise to do so, a brief review of the breadth and depth of the work handled by my companies — yes, today there are two Information Plus companies, the first one started in Canada and the affiliate located in the United States — is in order.

For over twenty years, my staff and I have researched companies in just about every state and province in North America, and overseas in Italy, the U.K., Australia, Thailand, Singapore, The Netherlands, Germany, and points in between. We have researched products as diverse as aggregates and chilled juices, high-voltage accessories and automobile tires, wedge connectors and fleece clothing, frozen novelty snacks, and smart cards. We've looked into service industries as varied as commercial housekeeping, interim hotel management, hazardous waste removal, technical writing, camera repair, and extended health care.

We've supported decisions about acquisitions, mergers, divestitures, market entries, market exits, lease renewals and equipment sales, overseas expansion and domestic renewal. We've done work to support companies' bids and tenders and also researched why certain companies didn't win contracts as expected. We've looked into the impact of acid rain on tourism and the pros and cons of electrical muscle stimulation in the weight loss business. We've gone behind the scenes to learn about companies, their products and markets, while keeping within the confines of what are considered ethical methods of information gathering.

We continue to work in industries ranging from pharmaceuticals, financial services, heavy manufacturing and retail to primary industries, electronics, hospitality, and utilities. In this continuing capacity, we've assisted Presidents and CEOs, Vice Presidents, Directors, and Managers. All of which informs the contents of this book. The examples quoted and the patterns observed are all based on real-world activity, although not all the cases cited are directly from the experience of Information Plus. Some examples are drawn from stories already in the public domain; the companies are well-known and their experiences have been documented in the press. In other cases, where the examples are based on projects handled between 1983 and 1998 (our records no longer go back to our inception) by Information Plus, company names have only been used on occasion and mainly when the companies profiled have made wise use of information in their decision making. When confidentiality agreements prevent the naming of names, no corporate identification has been given. Likewise, in the cases we know about where the client either ignored the research presented to them — or decided to forgo it in the first place — and suffered the consequences, names have not been used either, to protect both the innocent and the guilty!

This leads to perhaps the main impetus for writing this book and that is the very weak track record most North American companies still have when it comes to using information for decision making. Sadly, few really benefit from the wealth of what is available; even those with research staffs don't always get the full answers to their questions. The various causes of this state of affairs are discussed in this book. The outcome is that many business decisions turn out to be bad decisions and the reasons, in a nutshell, are that companies don't get the information that is readily available and the reason they don't is that they are not willing to spend the money to get it. How many times have I heard organizations making multi-millions of dollars a year say: "We have absolutely no market research budget." No market research budget? How will these folks fare in the Information Era of the 21st century? Not only should they have a market research budget — and a sizeable one at that — but they should also have a competitor research budget, a customer research budget, a lost customer research budget, a supplier research budget, a business development budget.... What these corporations don't understand is that, as information becomes increasingly important as the lifeblood of business, those companies that aren't investing heavily and regularly in information just won't be around in the future. The corporations with the best information — or even simply the better information — will have the tools with which to win.

Having talked in this way about what many companies don't have, it is perhaps timely to mention what this book does not offer. *Getting It Right: Avoiding the High Cost of Wrong Decisions* is not a book about critical thinking or decision-making skills, although it does touch on the tools of decision-making. It is not about organizational structure and how to design organizations to make decision-making easier. It doesn't cover every type of decision which has to be made, such as hiring decisions: there are already a number of books covering that particular topic. Rather, and given the author's strong track record in research in the business-to-business arena, it looks at decisions which companies must make concerning how their business will grow, expand, contract, compete or renew, decisions of a more strategic nature.

In this respect, *Getting It Right* fills a gap in the business literature. While there are other books about decision making — its processes, methodologies — none of them looks at the very close tie between having the right information and making the right decision. Even some of the so-called business "bibles," *In Search of Excellence, Competitive Strategy,* and others, while they discuss and dissect what companies do or what they ought to do, don't really look at this strong link between having the right information in hand *before* you make a decision as a predictor or prerequisite of having a desired outcome. And certainly none of the existing books look at the fact that companies, in the 21st century, will need to be proactive and gather information *they may end up not using.* Such thinking, of course, is anathema to many companies of the late 20th century. It also points up another fact which they will find equally disturbing: that there is a big difference between having an information *system* or IT and having good information *content.* It is information *content* which will decide the winners in the 21st century.

That leads me to another set of experiences which informs this book and that is my experiences as an employer over more than 15 years. In that time, I have had occasion to interview, hire, employ and, not infrequently, dismiss employees. And what sticks out like a sore thumb through all these experiences is just how woefully ill-trained many young people are for information *content* work. This situation does not improve with each passing year; with so much emphasis in the schools on the hardware of the computer and learning the skills for that, not enough attention has been paid to the skills needed to work with content which are nothing more than the good, old-fashioned "3Rs." Some of the problems this inappropriate emphasis in the schools has created are reviewed in various parts of this book. Educators may dispute the comments made, but for those of us out here "in the trenches," the view is perhaps a little more realistic than any held by an educator who does not have to correct the spelling mistakes and other errors of university graduates before work can be considered satisfactory for a paying customer. Should anyone still dispute this issue and ask why I think we have a basis for this conclusion, well, information *content* work is all we've ever done. What we do at Information Plus *is* the future!

Another observation, based on considerable experience over a number of years hiring people from a number of academic backgrounds and a range of countries, is that the skill sets, the background, which stand out as being the most valuable, the most relevant to working with information *content* (as opposed to systems and technology) — and the best predictor of success — are multilingual abilities. People, who can speak two or more languages well, take to information gathering and analysis the way a "duck takes to water"; others tend to flounder and drown. Failing that, a solid degree and ability in one's native tongue — in this case, an English degree — is the next best thing.

That this book is very timely was continually confirmed to me, even as writing progressed. Right up to the last minute, I kept finding corroboration and evidence to support many of the ideas set out in these pages. Article after article, in all manner of publications, stressed the various problems stemming from experimentation with educational systems, the damage done via Whole Language reading instruction in isolation from other methods, the wholesale pursuit of computers in the classrooms by school boards everywhere, all of which impair mental information processing and undermine good decision-making. Letters arriving in the mail at home, reminding me of a policy I had held with an insurer which collapsed, brought home the consequences of bad business decision making, as the letters reveal there is no money to pay me my premium refund claim!

Does this mean that I never make bad decisions myself? In the spirit of honesty the author of this book has to confess that she, too, in the past has made various bad decisions, not due to ignoring information or refusing to obtain it, but more usually from not getting enough information in hand. After posting year-over-year increases of 20 to 25% and having seen one of my companies grow 1300% in a 10-year period, in 1991, I leased very nice, Class A office space, armed with exciting plans for growth and business development. This move just happened to coincide with one of the worst and longest recessions in Canadian history, which left me scrambling to cover the rent for four years. (On the plus side, this did serve to spur me on to set up separate operations in the much larger and buoyant U.S. market, so we no longer have "all our eggs in one basket.") Then there's the condo I bought in 1987 which, had I known more about condos, I would not have bought the particular one I did. When there are only fifteen units in a condominium, the aggregate of common expenses does not provide an attractive opportunity to companies providing condo management. Net result: you have to take whichever manager you can get. Enough said!

The difference with these decisions, of course, is that they only affected a few people or just me personally; one of the points of writing this book is to help improve decisions made in business which affect hundreds if not thousands of people worldwide as corporate life becomes increasingly globalized.

If this book is the mirror of a long series of experiences, it is also something of a collective effort, as is everything we do at Information Plus. My thanks go to many people: first, to the many clients Information Plus has served since 1979 and without whose projects we would have neither the means to earn our living nor the insight to share in this book; to Kirk Tyson, for referring me to St. Lucie Press; and to Drew Gierman, at St. Lucie, for believing in this book. Thanks are also due to the great spin-on-a-dime research staff at my Canadian company, Milica Babic and Gordana Knezevic, along with Susan Michelmore at the U.S. company, for tracking down facts and confirming figures prior to publication, along with Katalin Egyed, at our Buffalo, NY office for diligently copying a wide selection of quotations about information and knowledge, so I could choose the best possible ones for each part of this book. Last but not least, thanks go to Linda Zangerle, also in my U.S. office, for inputting and outputting draft after draft of this manuscript as I polished it. Linda had to cope with increasingly deteriorating handwriting and sundry scribbles, not to mention manual cut-and-paste editing as the manuscript grew toward its finished form. Thanks also go to you, the reader, for buying this book and being open to taking a different approach to decision making, namely, getting it right!

Deborah C. Sawyer

About the Author

Deborah Sawyer is the President and founder of Information Plus, a firm providing value-added business research. In this capacity, Ms. Sawyer has been working with numerous clients across North America for 20 years, assisting them in finding the information they need to make better and more profitable decisions. Since its inception, Information Plus has worked with companies in the financial services, manufacturing, pharmaceutical, retail, food services, advertising, telecom, computer technology and utilities industries. The staff of Information Plus works on projects and ongoing monitoring assignments relating to clients' new business development, marketing, planning, competitive analysis, customer retention and prospect identification activities. Information Plus also custom builds databases for marketing, planning and other purposes.

A special focus of the firm is competitive intelligence (CI) gathering and analysis activities which have covered a broad spectrum of requirements: full profiles of competitor's organizations as well as investigations of specific areas such as distribution, sales, operations, service, marketing, new product development, pricing, costing, etc.

Information Plus now comprises two separate companies, one in Buffalo, NY, focusing on U.S. research, the other in Toronto, ON and focusing on Canadian research.

Prior to starting the company, Ms. Sawyer worked for three and a half years for an association, editing two reference books for the education field. She holds a Master's Degree in Library Science and a B.A. in Linguistics. Her languages include English and French fluently, with knowledge of Russian, German, Mandarin Chinese, and reading ability in Italian. She has travelled extensively, including the Far East, India, Malaysia, Singapore, Thailand,

North Africa, the former U.S.S.R., much of Europe, North and Central America, and the Caribbean and brings a global perspective to her work.

Deborah Sawyer also writes extensively on the subject of information, publishing a bi-monthly newsletter, *Information Solutions*, discussing intelligence-related topics of interest to business. She also writes on the subject of practice management for information services companies for *Information Broker*, an industry newsletter published in Houston, TX. She is the author of the books *Sawyer's Survival Guide for Information Brokers* and *Sawyer's Success Tactics for Information Businesses*, both published by Burwell Enterprises. On the subject of CI, Ms. Sawyer is also a regular contributor to the *Competitive Intelligence Magazine*, writing a column entitled "Defining Your Competition."

Information Plus also presents public seminars including "Customers: Analyzing the Hidden Dimension of Competition" and "Which League Do You Play In? How to Correctly Define your Competition to Maximize CI."

Ms. Sawyer also speaks frequently at conferences and seminars. In 1997, she presented a seminar at the SCIP conference in San Diego, addressed the Western New York International Trade Council, and spoke at CT–Expo in Atlanta. In 1998, she is already scheduled to speak at a meeting of the Buffalo/Niagara Sales & Marketing Executives, at the World Future Society conference in Chicago (July), at the American Society for Industrial Security in Dallas (September), at the Pricing Strategy conference presented by the Canadian Institute in Toronto (October) and at the Frost & Sullivan Growing Your Business conference in San Francisco (November). She has also been interviewed on radio and television.

1 Why Business Must Improve the Quality of Its Decisions

"There is only one good, knowledge,
and one evil, ignorance."
Socrates 469–399 BCE

Why Do We Need a Book about Business Decision Making?

How many times have you said "If only I'd known that, I'd never have"... bought that house/leased that car/taken that vacation/married that person... or a score of other past mistakes? All of us have, at one time or another in our personal lives, made decisions which later proved to be colossal mistakes. Some of these can be easy enough to overcome — hair dyed a strange color does grow out — while others turn out to be more serious errors: the marriage that didn't work out turns into the divorce-from-hell while the poor car choice consumes a king's ransom for repairs and maintenance.

But we usually learn from these mistakes and realize that, had we *known* more, been better informed, had access to more data at key times, we would have been able to avoid the situation. And so, the next time we face the same choices, we do take the steps to get the necessary information to make a better decision.

What is also key to remember about these personal choices is that the number of people affected are usually only a few. The poor decision about where to vacation affects maybe only one or two people at the most; an unwise house purchase may have an impact on four or five people. The range of damage for our personal decisions is usually small as concerns the number of people affected.

Not so in business. When a business decision maker makes a poor decision, hundreds, thousands, and perhaps even tens of thousands of people may suffer. As globalization changes the face of commerce, control over the careers of hundreds and hundreds of people rests in fewer and fewer hands. This suggests that business decisions have greater impact and need to be more carefully weighed.

Do Your Homework

Yet newspaper headlines daily suggest that the decisions being made in business are poor ones. "Hundreds of jobs lost" they scream. "Factory to close", "ABC Company files for bankruptcy," "Product X recalled worldwide."

It used to be that, prior to taking any action, a business person knew the maxim to follow was "do your homework." Finding out information and weighing the decisions to be taken were givens. The business press abounds with stories of economic and personal disaster for so many individuals, frequently revealing that business people are no longer "doing their homework."

Given that we live in a world where information is abundant to the point of overload, something seems to have gone terribly wrong. There isn't a shortage of information, so why have so many people stopped "doing their homework" before they make decisions?

This is one of the problems this book sets out to examine while also discussing how to put things right. By first looking at the emerging business environment of the 21st century and why business has to improve the quality of its decisions, we set the stage in Chapter 2 for examining the two main factors contributing to the problem: the way people make decisions and the information they have to make those decisions with.

This leads to a discussion in Chapter 3 of how business decisions are currently made and the "Seven Deadly Sins" of decision making. In Chapter 4, we get a better understanding of what information is and how to employ this tool to correct the problem. Steps to take with everyday business decisions are then reviewed in Chapter 5 while the implications of all this at the individual career level are then discussed in Chapter 6. We conclude in Chapter 7 by casting our eyes forward again, to the coming century, and see how this all fits together.

The Impending Crisis in Decision Making

Business is no more and no less than human beings acting together. But when just one business person makes the wrong decision, the consequences can be devastating for hundreds, thousands and even millions of other people, many of whom are no more than innocent bystanders.

Massive layoffs, numbering in the tens of thousands globally, can usually be traced back to faulty decision making by a handful of executives, years or even decades earlier. Accidents like Bhopal or the Exxon Valdez all stem from poor choices — in how to build and design a factory; how to staff the operation; in deciding what the goals of the undertaking should be.

Some people will shrug and say: Oh well, that's life! On balance, most businesses make the right decisions more often than the wrong. That may be true, and it may have been an acceptable approach in the past, but signs suggest that planet Earth and her inhabitants can no longer afford the impact of faulty decisions, even if they comprise only a quarter of the decisions made.

Decisions about plant locations, factory designs, manufacturing processes, waste treatment, and more must be the right ones, because we can no longer sustain the environmental damage when such decisions are wrong. Decisions about products, packaging, ingredients, and more, must be the right ones because we cannot afford the lawsuits, disabilities and suffering when they are wrong. Decisions about expansions at home or overseas must be the right ones, because we can no longer afford the social and economic costs of layoffs, family disintegration, and poverty when they are wrong.

Ripples on the Pond

Business decisions, often made on a "fly-by-the-seat-of-your-pants" basis, can have tremendous, far-reaching consequences. They are exactly like the pebble thrown into the middle of the pond which sends out ripple after ripple. The decision to build a plant in a small town and enjoy cheap labor along with low taxes is a poor decision if, a decade later, there are no solid reasons to remain in operation at that location and the factory is closed, leaving workers unemployed with no alternative jobs available. The ripples radiate quickly from the center of the pond — factory workers see their standard of living plunge, families must move or be separated as the bread-winner seeks work further afield, suppliers to the factory plus auxiliary businesses in the town see their revenues drop and may be faced with bankruptcy, property values plunge (not that anyone can sell their home) taxation to support government programs also drops, thereby causing deprivation further afield, crime escalates... and so, the ripples of damage spread. That's why everyone has an interest in better business decisions: workers, their families, business owners, shareholders, government officials, in fact, everyone who lives and breathes.

But while key decision makers in business, usually the senior executives but also managers lower down the company hierarchy, continue to commit one or more of the "Seven Deadly Sins" of business decision making, there will be no end to the ripples spreading on the pond.

Information Abundance

What is most sobering about this is that, all too often, better decisions could have been made, had the decision makers bothered to get the information that is *already readily available* and then bothered to pay attention to it.

While many people decry the proliferation of facts and figures which has led to so-called "Information Overload," this way of thinking obscures the reality: there is plenty of information available. We pay governments through our taxes to collect, synthesize, and disseminate information. Commercial publishers are motivated by the profit potential to assemble and disseminate information in a variety of forms: books, magazines, newsletters, databases, CD-ROMs, fax-alerting services, and more. Conference organizers and associations also get in on the act, gathering people together to share information, to publish it, and to store it. Universities and colleges also are creators and repositories of information. Then there are numerous commercial research companies which conduct a range of omnibus and syndicated studies to either distribute free or sell. In other words, in the free world of the westernized and industrialized nations, there is an abundance of information available, which can be had in many cases for free or at low cost.

And what is not readily available in this way can usually be assembled by conducting research studies to specifically target and gather the answers required. In fact, for most business decisions, up to 90% of the information required to make a sound decision can be found in either existing sources or at a modest cost, relative to the magnitude of the decision being made.

Abundance Creates Indifference

So why, then, has uninformed decision making been a stronger characteristic of the business world of the late 20th century than it should have been? Sometimes, abundance creates indifference, a tendency to take things for granted. Just as nations with abundant water resources become indifferent to this commodity, in contrast to many parts of the world where water is seen as a highly precious, almost revered treasure, business environments where information is abundant (and other resources such as money plentiful) tend to become careless, haphazard in how they use information in their decision making. People cite time pressures as one of the reasons not to look for information; coupled with this is frequently an unwillingness to pay anyone to look.

Even when companies do invest in information-gathering exercises to support their decision making, they are often hampered by a lack of reliable indicators to evaluate those who look for the information and their skills. Research is often delegated to those who fancy themselves as researchers, not necessarily to those who are best qualified by training and aptitude to handle the task. As *Getting it Right* explains, all this will have to change if businesses expect to survive through the next century.

The Business Environment of the 21st Century

Many predictions have been written about the business environment of the 21st century. People will work at home rather than in offices. Individuals will be self-employed rather than employees. All transactions will be over networks. Fewer hours will be worked and there will be more leisure time. Networks of fiber and silicon will replace those of tarmac and steel. Brains will become the "capital" rather than money. While some of these predictions will come true, many will not. But the one constant that seems to run through them all — and which will hold true — is that information will be *even more critical* to business and will form much more of the lifeblood of how business is done in the 21st century. How, then, will this affect the environment for decision making?

It is often overlooked that information has, in fact, always been important in business dating back into antiquity. The exchange of information has long been the crux of most business decisions and how people interact in business.

Going back in time to the marketplaces of antiquity, what you *knew* was as important then as it is today. Knowing that a caravan or ship with certain cargo was about to arrive was a lever for making money in the Middle Ages. By the time of the Renaissance and the first era of global expansion, knowing what minerals, crops, or other resources were available in distant lands allowed the entrepreneurs of the day to build their empires.

The so-called knowledge industries of the 20th century are really nothing new; in many cases, they are the same old activities dressed up in new clothes. All human activity is knowledge-based in some way. What has really changed and will be the hallmark of business in the 21st century is the level of attention paid to information and the importance assigned to it.

In this environment, it will be critical for companies who intend to remain in business and be profitable to obtain the best information *and* obtain *better* information than others in their industry. One of the stumbling blocks to this happening is that many people do not know good information from bad; the proliferation of sources of information over media such as the Internet has only worsened the picture. People are awash in a sea of information but do not have the skills to discern which information is valuable and which is worthless, many do not have the ability to tell accurate from inaccurate information, especially when it is available in computerized form; the automated nature of delivery somehow gives a benediction to everything transmitted this way meaning too many people have come to believe that *anything* coming out of the computer is infallible. This, sadly, is not the case. As anyone who has ever taken computer-based information and followed up on it will tell you, it is often hopelessly inaccurate and no more up-to-date than many print sources, the claims of producers of this electronic information notwithstanding.

The Importance of Information

Getting enough information and getting the best available will therefore be key success factors for all companies in the 21st century. But why don't companies follow these precepts now? Why, as late as the end of the 20th century, was the world still subject to the huge ripple effects of poor decision making?

Fear of Spending

The answer to that is simple. The reason costly mistakes are still made is that most companies are afraid to invest in getting information in the first place and are particularly afraid of investing in information they might not be able to use if the idea they are testing is shown to be a bad one by the information gathered. There seems to be a kind of perverse reaction which takes hold; many companies, even sizeable ones with deep pockets, will shy away from shelling-out $20,000 to invest in some research about a new product idea, an acquisition, or business expansion overseas, but will happily plunge ahead with their scheme and rack up a $20 million loss when it turns out to be a dud. The poet Goethe once wrote "Fortune favors the bold" but this is not the same as saying fortune favors the reckless. Many shareholders of publicly traded companies would be horrified if they knew of the losses occurring at the companies in which they hold shares, precisely because of reckless and uninformed decision making.

An equal factor in this poor decision-making phenomenon is the extent to which companies do not turn outside for information but restrict the gathering of facts to support critical new ventures to their in-house staff. This tactic is employed because it is safer, less threatening for the decision makers. Since it is very unlikely that people working in a company are going to present information which could put them out of a job, all information gathered internally to support decision making, needs to be viewed with skepticism. Only a handful of companies, as late as the end of the 20th century, were willing to invest in both internally gathered information *as well as* externally gathered, both of which are equally important.

Lessons From the Past

This suggests another fundamental change, which will have to occur, is in how companies perceive expenditures on information. There was a time, back before advertising or public relations became as widely used as they are, when companies would bitch about having to spend on such "soft" costs, on an intangible like an ad in a magazine or a press release.

Organizations have now moved through their learning curves on such components of a successful operation so there is less resistance than there once was. The same has yet to happen with information. Companies which don't yet invest heavily in information gathering will have to get started; even those who currently do will have to ramp up to a higher level. This will likely be accompanied by a fair amount of squawking, but when they see the impact on the bottom line, the squawking will die away. Multimillion dollar losses attributable to ignoring often readily available information will have no place in the Information Era of the 21st century.

The Value of Good Thinking Skills

How then can companies ensure that they are getting this good information that is so critical in making the right decisions? A lot of this has to do with the human resources at a company and the type of thinking skills such employees can use.

Finding information — the right information — requires good detective skills. The ability to raise a broad spectrum of perceptive and varied questions, to follow-up on clues (much the way police detectives follow-up on stray hairs and fingerprints) are all the foundation of getting the right information and avoiding the wrong decisions.

Much like solving any puzzle, those who are able to do good detective work will win out over those who do sloppy detective work. This analogy to detectives is very apt; the resources available to solve a crime will determine if the criminals get caught or not. Put another way, if you have to get murdered, it is best to have this happen in a big city rather than in a rural area. There is a greater likelihood that your murderer will be caught in a large metropolitan area where police departments have a lot of resources and a lot of people with their combined thinking skills, to draw upon. In the 21st century, the companies with the best "detectives" will be the ones who continually turn up the winners. Those companies staffed by people with weaker "detective skills" will either have to turn to outside sources to supplement their in-house resources or will go under.

This is because detective work depends on someone's ability to pull a situation apart and analyze it from all angles. To give a business example, consider how, in the last five years, more than one bagel chain in the United States has run into financial difficulty. It seems there were just too many of these places relative to the population's demand for bagels. But some of these chains were owned by considerably larger enterprises who, one assumes, had a lot of resources to draw upon. Perhaps these companies had a lot of tangible resources but possibly did not employ the best thinkers. The rampant expansion of bagel chains failed to consider, for example, the fact that bagels are also sold in supermarkets and that supermarkets are a form of competition. Not everyone wants to stop on the way to work to buy a bagel nor do they want to go in and sit down at a coffee and bagel place to eat one. The thinkers also seemed to overlook the fact of the aging population and changing trends in diet. People who are no longer going to work because they are retired may be less interested in going out to eat a bagel when they can buy some and have them right at home; health problems — food allergies, medical conditions, obesity — are another reason that customers may not have been buying in the droves that were anticipated. Had the companies setting up the bagel chains had better "detectives" on their staffs, they may have looked at enough different issues and asked enough of the right questions to get the right information in and therefore make better decisions, such as choosing another line of business.

Better Decisions as Career Insurance

That the impact of a bad decision is felt at more than the overall organization level is not hard to guess. It doesn't take much of a genius to recognize that when companies make bad decisions, some of the repercussions usually include layoffs. This suggests that, in the business environment of the 21st century, learning how to make better decisions can be key career insurance, for individuals, whether they work for themselves or someone else. Anyone who can seriously reduce if not eliminate the number of wrong decisions they make as part of their work stands a greater chance of enjoying ongoing employment. To do this, of course, you need to recognize good information over the not-so-good, not always an easy task given the amount of "junk information" that is already circulating out there. One of the objectives of this book is to pass along some of the professional know-how to guide readers to being able to discern the good from the bad in the information that comes their way. The aim is also to share the techniques of being able to seek out and requisition good from bad information when using outside suppliers for the task of gathering it. While no one can guarantee that you will never make a bad decision, reading this book and putting the recommendations into practice will ensure that very few of the decisions you make are the wrong ones.

Selected References

"Blinded by the Byte," *Forbes ASAP*, February 24, 1997, p. 22.
Competitive Strategy, The Free Press/Macmillan Publishing, 1980, 396 pp.

"Corporate Decision Making," *The Economist*, September 8, 1990, p. 76-77 [excerpted in "Media Watch" in *Focus*, November 1990, newsletter of the Toronto Chapter of The Planning Forum (now Strategic Leadership Forum)].

"Don't Forget: Garbage in, Garbage out," *Computer World Canada*, October 8, 1993, p. 12.

"The Downside of Downsizing," *Business Week*, April 28, 1997, p. 26.

"Information Superhighway," *Executive Excellence*, April 1995, p. 15.

In Search of Excellence, Harper & Row, 1982, 360 pp.

"Interhooey," *Forbes*, May 5, 1997, p. 176.

"Love'em or Lead'em: So You Think Your Workers Want a Boss They Can Like? Better Think Again," *Canadian Business*, April 10, 1998, p. 120.

"Prediction's Accuracy No Solace to Engineer [Boliden Disaster], *Globe & Mail*, May 2, 1998, p. A16.

"Seek Truth on the Web," *Information World*, March 3, 1997, p. 94.

2 The Knowledge Economy: How the Importance of Decision Making Will Increase

"Knowledge is of two kinds. We know a subject ourselves or we know where we can find information upon it."
Samuel Johnson, 1775

When people in business sit down to make decisions, they have two basic tools at their disposal: their own brains and whatever information they have been able to gather to support their decision making.

Their brain resources include their training and education, their experiences and beliefs, their biases, and their intuition. On the information side of the equation, they may have an abundance of material at hand or, if they lack the resources or know-how to retrieve good information, they may have very little.

The emergence of the so-called Knowledge Economy is starting to place an increasingly greater premium on brains as capital. While information or knowledge has long been the underpinning of all human endeavor, as the role of information in business takes on greater importance, "brain capital" as it's usually called, swims into the spotlight. And, what is often found upon examination, is that a lot of this brain capital is not up to the task, for reasons which we'll discuss.

The other half of the decision-making equation is information or, more precisely, what people perceive as information and how they use it. Misunderstandings about information: its quality, its reliability, its accuracy along with an unwillingness, by vast numbers of businesses, to invest in what they see as a "soft" cost, is a further factor which has been undermining decision-making in the latter part of the 20th century.

There are indications that the very abundance of information has created indifference to its use as a tool in decision making. People seem to avoid using it at the very times when information could prevent a business from setting off on a perilous course. Later in this book, we will look at some of the reasons for making such excuses and how to stop this practice.

Brains as Capital: One Half of the Equation

Although talk about the transition from an industrial economy to a knowledge-based economy is plentiful, such speculation fails to look at the full implications of what this transition brings.

In the old industrial economy, you could actually see the capital: money in the bank, machinery on the shop floor, head counts of labor. Even better, you could see how these elements of capital worked together. It was possible to see if the interactions were good or not and easy to see that the right processes were being used to produce the right outcomes. Just about everything that was the "guts" of the industrial economy's workings was out in the open.

The New Capital

Fast-forward to the late 1990s and the emergence of what is called the Knowledge Economy. The old capital of money, machinery, and labor is on the way out; the new capital of human brain power is on the way in. But how do you *see* how this new capital works? It is not yet possible to peer into the human brain to see how it stores, processes and utilizes knowledge. It is not even possible to see what knowledge people really have as opposed to what they say they know. Nor can you easily assess how they make decisions.

Outward indicators are of no help in assessing these factors. Any number of people have college degrees. But does this mean they are all equally well-educated? Far from it; the colleges they attended, the nature of the courses they sat through, the quality of their professors, the discipline in their learning environments, can differ tremendously, meaning a college degree is no indicator of how well-educated someone is or how much knowledge they have.

Even within a group of graduates who have sat through identical programs, resulting knowledge levels will differ wildly. Human memory is very selective. The ability of individuals to retain information is also varied. As a result, a crop of graduates from the exact same MBA course will not all be equally valuable to business. Some will have little or no real ability to integrate the different aspects of their learning nor will they be able to correctly apply what they have learned.

Because of these tremendous variations in how individuals synthesize and then analyze knowledge, there is no way to see how people are making decisions and whether they have made their decisions in the right way or not. Businesses therefore currently rely on externals — such as academic degrees, which are *not* very reliable for this purpose — to select decision-makers for their organizations. And the process will be a hit-and-miss affair until better assessment methods arise and better training in decision making is available, meaning many enterprises will be left vulnerable to the poor decisions people in charge will make. This vulnerability to poor decisions has always been a problem for businesses but it is the evolution of a knowledge economy, where information is more critical than it has been historically, that makes winning or losing rest more heavily than ever before on which decisions are made and how they are made.

The very great danger in the era of the knowledge economy is that brain capital is largely invisible, currently unmeasurable and, if faulty, absolutely lethal.

Brain — Not Information — Overload

Another invisible but equally important factor to be considered, in any discussion of brain capital, is what the human brain can process over the course of a day. While Information Overload may be the reigning buzzword, the real underlying problem is Brain Overload. Even the best-educated minds can only process about 150 words a minute, regardless of whether these words appear on the printed page or computer screen. This has changed relatively little since the 15th century, when the invention of movable type printing press ushered in the so-called Gutenberg Era.

So even when the brain capital at a company looks to be the very best, at least on the surface, it is still constrained by the realities of Mother Nature, as to how quickly information can be processed. And if there are decision makers in a business who process information at a rate less than 150 words a minute, there is a great danger they will short-circuit the process and skip the input of critical information altogether. If a company has decision makers who skip such key parts of the decision-making process because their brain capital is weak in this respect, the company will be on a collision course with disaster.

National Education Systems and the Advantage of Nations

To understand more about how brain capital can be an "Achilles Heel" for business and why decision making, based on poor brain capital, is such a high-risk proposition, we need to go back to look at the underpinning of decision making which really starts in a person's first days of life, but certainly can be traced to the beginning of their schooling. The schools are still the primary vehicle for shaping the mind and it is the way the mind is being trained which determines how effective or otherwise someone is as a decision maker.

The historical model of schooling rested on uniformity and exposure, during the compulsory school years, to a fairly standardized curriculum. These were the days when people had to learn to do mathematics without a calculator, where spelling without a spell checker was mandatory, and where higher education rested on the fundamentals of a lot of rote learning in the lower grades. By the time someone graduated from high school, they would have been exposed to a battery of fairly standard and predictable subject matter. Certain assumptions could be made about what they had been taught.

The current model, particularly in North America, is less uniform. It is marked by a distrust of rote learning and a belief in freedom of expression for the student, which has often come to mean that anything a student produces is praised as the work of a unique human being without due attention to how it would stand up under scrutiny of a wider audience. Students are also given more and earlier freedom to choose their curriculum of study, meaning fewer and fewer people are graduating from high school with consistent exposure to mathematics, physics, chemistry, history and geography, which are deemed to be "boring." Likewise, learning foreign languages or how to play a musical instrument are seen by many students as requiring too much effort.

The net result of this can actually be broken down into four components. The first is that there is no standard anymore, and it cannot be assumed that high-school graduates know certain basics, something employers are frequently discovering to their horror, when they find young people cannot write a coherent letter, cannot spell correctly, cannot do mental arithmetic, and have a very shaky knowledge of geographic place names, in their own country much less elsewhere in the world. All very fine and dandy, except if you're an exporter dealing with clients overseas or a business serving a nation-wide customer-base, this sort of thing can prove a source of embarrassment.

The second element is that this free-for-all in the schools, allowing unfettered choice of subjects of interest and too much tolerance for whatever work an individual student produces, is that standards have become lower. Why else are so many universities forced to offer courses in remedial English to teach new undergraduates, native speakers of English, how to write and spell correctly, so they can cope with their workload? The fact the lack of uniformity and standards has done damage to students' thinking ability is further evidenced by comments from university professors, teaching in all parts of the continent, who notice that today's freshmen often have difficulty understanding standard texts in introductory courses which have been used for many years and did not similarly faze the freshmen of earlier decades. If first-year university students of the late 20th century cannot grasp the fundamentals, it does not promise that their decision-making skills will be very sound when they enter the work force.

It also remains to be seen what other impact there will be from the experiment with reading instruction known as Whole Language. While this method may be an appropriate *complement* to the older, more traditional phonics, there is evidence to suggest Whole Language methods should not be used in isolation from phonics and that one of the resulting outcomes is a number of young people, multiple generations in fact, who have impaired mental information processing abilities as a result. Put another way, while most people from the Victorian era would not have had trouble processing and comprehending the lengthy sentence immediately preceding this one, many of today's school children and even college students will have difficulty; this does not bode well for a world where many Information Era or Knowledge Economy jobs will revolve around the ability to process textual information and interpret it.

This leads to a third element of this situation namely, that young people today often lack strong memories. An educational system which allowed itself to disparage rote learning is one that unfortunately forgot the mind is like a muscle and needs to be trained. The memorization of multiplication tables, historical dates, pieces of poetry and songs, and other subject matter during the early school days lays the foundation for a sharp mind later in life. Allowing students to graduate from high school without this mental training, telling them that they can rely on the computer or the calculator to do their brain work, doesn't just do them a disservice, it does the whole of society a disservice.

All of which leads to the final and most unfortunate aspect of this: not all countries have experimented in this fashion with their school systems. While some of the conditions in schools overseas, where university entrance is a highly competitive (sometimes even a suicidal) affair, are not to be emulated, some aspects should. Schools with disciplined learning environments tend to produce individuals with disciplined minds. This does not mean they are uncreative; the most creative person in the world will likely never achieve much if they are not also disciplined. But those people with better trained minds, with the ability to retain facts, are those who are better positioned to synthesize and then extrapolate from this information. Such skills are the foundation of good decision making. Those nations which still have work forces of well-disciplined minds will be those that have an advantage over those which do not.

As You Think, So Will You Earn

This suggests that some people, more than being predisposed by natural ability, are predisposed by training to be better thinkers and therefore better decision makers. Facts are the crux of thinking and decision making. Otherwise, it is easy for anyone who wants to bamboozle you, to do so. Top-notch lawyers do not generally win cases because they are continually running to their notes or their laptop computers to look things up; they are able to discredit witnesses and spot errors and inconsistencies in testimony, simply because they have good memories which can tuck this sort of information away, ready to pull out when needed.

Good doctors don't diagnose what is wrong with their patients by rummaging around in books or scrolling through computer screens. Their minds have to be well-disciplined repositories of information which they sometimes supplement with aids such as books and CD-ROMs.

The importance of a good memory even shows up in what might be termed less intellectual occupations. Few people would have much confidence in their local fire departments if, while their house burns, the firefighters are busy booting up their computers to see how to deal with the blaze!

In the Knowledge Economy, a well-trained mind will be essential both to personal success and as the foundation of better decisions. Those who can consistently make good decisions will be those who are in demand for permanent employment. Those who can use information as a tool in this way and can largely do so from the foundation of mind, not from the screen of a computer, will be those who are quick enough on their feet to have value in running organizations of all sizes. This is not to suggest that a good memory relieves you of the necessity of checking the facts; rather, it is the tool which raises a red flag when things don't add up. Those whose memories are so poor that they cannot even remember the name of the customer they spoke with on the phone an hour ago will face even more uncertain futures than they do today.

Assessing Brain Capital

How can companies therefore go about assessing the brain capital they employ? What tools can be used for this purpose? How can human resources personnel unravel a job applicant's thought processes?

While there are unquestionably a lot of psychological tests and various measures of raw ability which can be taken into consideration, there are, as yet, few real tools which can be used to determine how an individual thinks, how they process information, and how they extrapolate from it. This situation is further muddied by the fact that there is not always a single solution to problems in business but more than one path to the solution, although the outcome might be the same in each case. The way individuals approach decision making is therefore not rigidly standardized as to process, although it may need to be standardized as to outcome. For example, how someone thinks through the desirability of an acquisition, the necessity of a market exit, the timing to launch a new product, etc. can follow various routes to reach a good decision. There may not be a single path although the decision taken still needs to be the right one.

Until testing instruments catch up with the knowledge economy, companies may still have to rely on a bit of trial-and-error in assessing their brain capital, by hiring people and giving them low-risk decisions to make, to determine how they operate, before allowing them to take on the higher-risk decisions. This is essentially how a lot of organizations have functioned historically but with the imperative to use information more actively as a tool in business as the 21st century unfolds, some of this trial and error method will take too long and so other approaches will be needed.

To this end, companies will have to look into the backgrounds of job candidates and people already on-board more closely. Where an individual took *all* their schooling, not just college, but primary and secondary education as well, will become a key point of analysis. What were the schools like? What were the teachers like? Anyone who can remember their early grade school report cards, with gems of advice such as "needs to pay more attention to detail" or "needs to apply him- or herself more" will remember the old adage "the child is the father of the man." Such shortcomings, if not addressed, can dog that individual's career through life. Such comments, however long ago they were written, are often excellent indicators of how well someone will do their information work as an adult.

An individual's activities will also be an indicator of how well-trained their minds are and how solid their memory is. People who regularly took place in debates, who have participated in choirs, bands and dramatic presentations, probably have memories which are better trained than the average person. The same is true of people who have studied foreign languages and can actually retain and speak these languages, especially some time after studying them. The people who are still good at mental arithmetic as opposed to those who rely on the calculator, probably have more active memories than those who always need a mechanical crutch. Those who participate in pastimes such as chess may indicate a good depth of memory and the ability to process complex thoughts.

Information Skills

Companies will also need to be able to assess more quickly, which job candidates as well as current employees really do possess the kind of "detective skills" referenced earlier which are the foundation of information work. Raw curiosity is not enough; abilities are needed above and beyond this. Good information workers definitely need the strong memories discussed in this chapter, even to the point of having photographic memories and strong visual recall. The ability to notice patterns in behaviors and events and then spot the breaks in the patterns are essential. The ability to make connections between seemingly unrelated events — and be right about it — is fundamental. The ability to decipher "codes" which may manifest as verbal, visual, or auditory clues is another key attribute. The ability to move from a multiplicity of complex causes to their effects is essential. And the ability to encode the results into presentations so everyone can understand them is also vital.

Lifelong Learning: The Critical Investment

As information, its accumulation, transfer, interpretation, and exploitation become the principal levers of business transactions, individuals will need to invest even more than today in lifelong learning. Those who take courses, invest in disciplined, sequential study leading to certificates, those who travel, especially to other countries, will have the enriched minds for a business economy heavily dependent on information. Building more layers of knowledge will be as fundamental an investment practice as is salting away funds for retirement.

Adding to this problem, in the knowledge or information era, will be what happens to peoples' minds and their abilities to make decisions when the information they put in their heads during their own time is not quality information. It is up to the reader to speculate what sort of thinker a person will be who fills their own time with soap operas, talk and game shows, surfing pornographic sites on the Internet, and similar pursuits. Do these activities improve the mental resource of the individual? As was suggested above, in the 21st century, even more than today, it will be those who enrich their understanding of the world and otherwise build layers of enrichment in their minds who will be the most sought after in terms of their decision-making ability in a world increasingly dependent on information.

The Other Half: The Right Information At The Right Time

Learning may be the key to earning — or better thinking and decision-making skills — but it is only one half of the decision-making equation. The other half is information, particularly the right information at the right time.

If Today's Information had been Yesterday's Machinery, Half the Factories Would Have Closed

The industrial economy of yesterday hummed and grew because people continued to find ways to build more and better machinery. The impulse to improve on the machinery already developed came from many directions but once people had achieved such a state-of-the-art they could *see* the results of their efforts. They *knew* they had achieved quality.

In the knowledge or information economy, there are few, if any, outward indicators that a pinnacle of quality has been reached inside someone's head. The "machinery" of decision making, which is an interplay of memory and other cognitive processes in the brain with inputs of external information, is not visible. It is only from someone's outward actions and the results of those actions, which often have a long-term horizon to realization, that the quality of the individual's thought processes and decision making can be revealed. Whereas with machinery, a prototype can be built or a process can be run on a test scale, there is no way of conducting a realistic trial with someone's decision to buy a company, enter or exit a market, expand overseas, etc.

Compounding this problem is the availability of information used to make business decisions and its quality. If the information that is often currently used to underpin business decisions, if this part of the "machinery" which drives current decision making, were the actual or real machinery of the industrial era, then half the factories would have shuddered to a halt. And the other half would likely have just croaked along. *That's because the information being used for decision making often is not quality information.* If it was real, physical machinery, very little of it would work.

The Discipline of Information Expertise

As of the late 20th century, people from all types of background were using information and believing they had the expertise to find and use it without any formal training in the discipline of information.

Many people are exposed to using libraries while in school or college but never really master how to use such repositories. The techniques for searching online databases are not taught in a systematic way; many users learn by a "hunt-and-peck" method. Few people are ever taught about the creation of information: who has the motives to compile data and what bearing this may have on availability and quality. That all public domain information, such as that found in libraries or on databases, is the outcome of deliberate efforts, does not seem to enter into the typical information user's frame of reference. A situation where the untrained are allowed unrestricted access to information, to do with it as they please, is a bit like letting kids loose in the proverbial candy store.

This lack of information discipline and related problems is what is troubling about the second half of the decision making equation.

No Quick Fixes

There is also the fact that people who are untrained in information work believe there is a magic button or some quick fix they can rely on. "Tell me the Top 10 sources of information I can use " they say, thinking that once they know these, they'll be set for life. The danger, if such people do find a list or a book, even one with considerably more than ten sources, is that this becomes a crutch. They latch on to this and stop thinking creatively. The fact the sources need to be selected relative both to the information needed and the decisions to be made doesn't seem to occur to them nor does it seem to occur that what is an ideal source for one set of questions may actually be a bad source for another situation.

A further shortcoming of the uninitiated, and this includes many executives and managers, is that they set deadlines for meetings or timetables for making a decision and then set about requesting the information. In many such cases, the timeframe available is not adequate to the task. Two weeks is not enough for an information gathering mission, starting from scratch, to support a major new product initiative or a market entry. In many cases, neither is four weeks, nor six weeks. Nor eight. But this is how such decisions are made, completely on a rush basis. What the repercussions of this methodology are will be examined in Chapter 3 while how long a search should take will be discussed in Chapter 4.

Even when the information-gathering process goes smoothly, those untrained in information work often fail to recognize that once gathered, the data is only a starting point. Time is usually needed to get information out of the data, again by those all-important thinking processes. Requiring people to make snap decisions when a company may have to live with the consequences for a decade or more does not lay the foundation for continued success and profitability.

The Mirage of Information Systems

Compounding this deception nowadays is a belief, held by many in large organizations, that their employers' computer systems and the internal information on those systems have all the answers. Few organizations are really so self-sufficient in information. To understand the danger of this thinking, consider the analogy between a company's computer system or network and the plumbing in your own house. No doubt at home you have a full array of pipes, faucets, and valves but if there is no water flowing through those pipes, they are as good as useless. Or, if the water coming out of your taps is not safe to drink, it is of no value to you. This is often true of a company's internal information systems, great "pipes" but lousy "liquid;" those who rely heavily on internally generated information and all the biases that this type of information is heir to run the risk of finding the information inadequate. External information, such as that about competitors and customers, is inadequately represented in the internal mix at the best of times. The sophistication of the technology lulls everyone into a false sense of security, believing that their IT will always have the answers they need.

Availability Does Not Equal Quality

Then, in the general trumpeting about the availability of information over networks such as the Internet, many people overlook the fact that availability of information is not the same thing as quality of information. Even when the vast amount of pornographic material is subtracted from the mix, much of what proliferates over the Internet and in many other sources is repetitive, worthless "junk" information. Sources of information about publicly traded companies are a "dime a dozen" whereas data about privately held companies is scarce. Information about regulated industries proliferates whereas there is far less available about unregulated enterprises. Some information, such as about faulty products, may even be suppressed.

Then, information available via the Internet or in commercial on-line databases is no less heir to being inaccurate, out-of-date or incomplete than its print equivalent. Such information is often incorrectly indexed, with inappropriate keywords assigned, causing a user to wade through irrelevant material to obtain what is needed. Even worse, an increasing amount of this material is really "disinformation," information deliberately created by one party to deceive, mislead, or intimidate one or more other parties. It is known that disgruntled ex-employees, for example, create bogus Web sites as part of a plan of revenge. (Few people tapping these sites bother to read the disclaimers). As the era of networks and the Internet advances, this problem will escalate with often serious repercussions for businesses which rely on these sources to the exclusion of others.

The Downward Trend

And in spite of the proliferation of information brought to the world by the Internet and the World Wide Web, there are indications that availability of all types of information, regardless of the format, is actually deteriorating. While computer-based sources have mushroomed there has often been a contemporaneous loss of comparative sources of information, a trend which has already transformed printed published information. At one time, in any given industry, there would be three or four of what's known as "industry bibles," directories, trade magazines and the like, which people could rely on. The economies of publishing have, in recent years, reduced the number of such "bibles" to one per industry. It doesn't take long in a world without competition for quality to drop. The level of detail of information drops along with attention to detail; proofreading errors mushroom as available data dwindles. This means that sources once considered reliable can no longer be considered so.

Even governments have felt the pinch as the costs of information compilation have soared. Once, sources like the Department of Commerce, and its counterparts in other developed countries, produced extensive data but rationalization has occurred with many key sources, such as the Census, being scaled back. At one time, the range of questions asked produced finely detailed breakdowns of industry and market data. A comparison of what was produced 30 or 40 years ago to work published today, however excellent it is, quickly shows up the drop in quality. Questions are dropped from the Census as budgets tighten. This leaves regular users of Census material lamenting the loss of data. Another phenomenon in such centrally collected statistics is the emergence of the NEC (Not Elsewhere Classified) category as newer or more esoteric products and industries are lumped together, in broad, often useless, categories of data. Funds just aren't available to document them all in detail.

Happily for the publishers of such material — and unhappily for businesses which need accurate decisions made — the skills to double check such information and tap multiple sources to support decision making are in decline, thanks to changes in the education system. As cited in the previous chapter, one of the first tests of accuracy and authenticity, a good memory, is no longer available to many. Again, good memory cannot be the only source tapped but it is a terrific guidepost to avoiding the false, the inaccurate, the scam. Knowledge of alternative sources, when such do exist, is weak. There is strong evidence to suggest that the current generation graduating from school not to mention younger people already in the workforce, have a profound and naive belief in the computer. To them, any information generated from a computer source is reliable, accurate and not to be questioned. Text printed in newspapers which would be treated with skepticism by many informed readers in its paper form, is suddenly transformed into the "gospel truth" when it is produced from a computer database. This does not augur well for business decision making.

The rush by schools everywhere to load up their classrooms with computers is also doing damage in another way; what seems to be forgotten in this lemming-like pursuit of technology is that learning how to push the right keys on a computer keyboard does not prepare students for higher level thinking or problem-solving. There is no difference between training people to punch Function Key 7 and training them to tighten screw number 59 on the production line at the factory. Both are shortcuts to a mental ghetto.

The author has also seen too many examples of people in their twenties who worship the computer, the current "god du jour," and cannot or will not question the validity of the information found this way, much of which is inaccurate.

Land of Hype and Glory

Another factor complicating the ability of those untrained in information work to source information for decision making, is the way sources of information are marketed. Every time a new database or a new search engine for the Web or even a new print publication makes its appearance, the positioning in the promotional materials is that of: "this is all you will ever need."

The producers of such information know, all too well, that humans want it easy, so they hype their service or product to present it as a "one-stop shopping" experience. While it is hoped many educated people can see beyond the marketing pitch, some recent evidence of business decision making with its environmental damage, mass layoffs, plant closures and the like, suggests many people do not. Perhaps this phenomenon is the modern equivalent for the quest for the Holy Grail? The "eureka... I've found it" euphoria takes hold, meaning far too many people are blindsided by the hype.

The Trap of Question Migration

What is also at work here is a combination of this human laziness with inertia and procrastination. It is much easier to rely on easily available information or a company's internal systems for the information they make available than it is to go and look for fresh answers. It is even easier to start migrating one's questions to fit these readily available answers, which is another way of believing you already have all the answers.

Question migration is something of a step child of Information Overload; someone sets out, with the best of intentions to gather information to support a market entry decision or to direct new product development and then downloads a stack of articles from the computer. When there is such quantity available, it is discouraging to think it might not provide any quality. As the information seeker moves through the stack — which takes time — the mind starts to play tricks. (After all, after two or three hours of poring over the documents, who wants to pronounce the exercise futile and start over?) An "it'll do" mentality surfaces, meaning dubious facts and figures are now anointed as being the right information. What is really at work is an unfortunate process of metamorphosis, as the key questions the company has identified as necessary to success are reshaped and realigned to fit the material at hand.

Many companies practice question migration, rather than face up to the fact they don't really have the information they need.

The Perils of Poor Information

This suggests that the decline in information quality, coupled with a lack of skills to double check sources, makes a vast number of business decision makers vulnerable to making the wrong decision, perhaps even more so than the immediate generations which preceded them. At the same time, in the 21st century, the pivotal nature of information as a support to making the right decision will increase. As mentioned in part one, on a world with a burgeoning population and increasingly fragile environment, the impact of the wrong decision cannot be as readily absorbed. In a global economy, the shock waves from a wrong decision made at corporate headquarters in one part of the planet can affect people in many, many other parts. Does this mean all information is poor? Far from it — as stated earlier, most decisions which turn out to be bad could have been avoided, had the decision makers bothered to tap the wealth of readily available information. What is often not discernible to the untrained eye, is the readily available information which can be relied upon and that which should be discarded as unreliable. It is this gap — between the quality information and that which is just dross — which this book also attempts to address.

A State of Unreadiness

Few companies, in the late 20th century, have the mechanisms to deal with this convergence of undertrained decision makers with the concurrent burgeoning of poor-quality information.

Another limitation is the perception, held by many organizations, even multibillion dollar corporations, that expenditures on information content (as opposed to information systems and technology) are a waste of money.

Ironically, it is the companies which place the most emphasis on IT which will be at a disadvantage as the Information Era, the era of content, unfolds. Large staffs who can write good code are not necessarily equipped to switch to the often ephemeral world of content which is frequently characterized by ambiguities, contradictions, and unknowns. These companies may well find they have sizeable headcounts to lay off — in itself a sign of poor decision making based on ignoring available information in the late 20th century. Code is only useful for pushing the content around the system; the ability to write code is often at odds with being able to process and analyze a lot of "real-world" data.

How Much To Invest In The Search

One of the reasons that companies don't currently invest more in information is that it is hard to obtain yardsticks as to how much to invest and what a fair price is for a piece of research.

One of the best rules of thumb in such cases is to look at what expenditure is proportionate to the activity or, what is the likely cost of not investing in information gathering and research. For example, a major acquisition with a price tag of $500 million, whether being handled as an LBO or as a stock swap or a cash outlay, probably is worth an investment of at least $50,000. The $50,000 represents just .001% of the purchase price but some companies will still say that's too much, especially if the acquisition does not go through.

Such companies are those which have not yet made the mind-shift to the Information Era, when such expenditures will not only become necessary but managers and others may be held liable by shareholder groups, unions and others for not making them. If this sounds far-fetched, a useful analogy is the environmental arena, where companies now today regularly have to invest in audits and assessments and in maintaining their facilities in compliance to environmental standards. Once upon a time, no one voluntarily undertook such expenditures and so the legislative environment changed into one requiring it. While it is unlikely that legislation would require companies to invest more in information to back their decisions — although this might not be unheard of for large publicly traded companies — it is more likely that moral suasion or other external influences will necessitate such investments.

Investing regularly in up-to-date and current information should therefore be an ongoing expenditure, whether based on a percentage of a company's revenues, proportionate to the long-term costs of ventures undertaken or gauged in some other way relative to the company's activities. Obviously, the decision to purchase paper clips does not require any real investment in an information search, other than perhaps using office supplies catalogs to comparison shop. But as the significance of the decision increases relative to the company's long-term well being, so should the willingness to invest dollars increase.

Selected References

"Check E-mail Sources," *Information Week*, October 14, 1992, p 126.

"Critical Thinking to Improve Your Strategic Odds" [speech] T. Quinn Spitzer at SCIP Conference, Chicago, IL, March 1998. Tapes available by contacting SCIP at (703)739-0696.

"Get Your Facts Here," *Forbes*, March 23, 1998, p. 156.

"Futurist Sees Changes for IT Industry Workers," *Computer World*, November 5, 1993.

"Harness the Technology," *Information Week*, February 17, 1997, p. 88.

"I Rarly Writed More Then a Paragraphs [sic]," *Globe & Mail*, September 26, 1995.

"Information has Become a Form of Garbage," *Globe & Mail*, November 25, 1993, p. [16].

"Information Rage," *Financial Post*, April 16, 1998, p. 19.

" 'Literacy Requires Phonics and Whole Language,' Dean says," *Purdue News*, April 1998, p. 2–3.

"Meet the N-generation," *Report on Business Magazine*, November 1997, p 142.

"Our Kids Have 'Self-Esteem' — They Just Can't Add or Subtract," *Financial Post*, November 30, 1996.

"Readin,' Writin' and... Rachmaninoff?" *Canadian Business*, July 1996, p. 73.

"Scientists Need Not Apply [school curriculum]," *Forbes*, March 23, 1998, p. 66.

"Smelling the Tulips," *Information Week*, July 22, 1996, p. 100.

"Stagecoach Days on the Info Highway," *Forbes ASAP*, 1997, p. 25.

"Super Egos [grade inflation]," *Marketing Tools*, August, 1997, p. 64.

"Technology: Reflections on a God that Failed," *Toronto Star*, July 24, 1993, p. E6.

"The Three Big Lies of Computers and Schools," *Canadian Business*, September 1997, p. 115.

"Tired of 'Spoon-Feeding' Your Employees? [ad]" placed by CEO America, Bentonville, AR 501/273-6957.

"Weak Literacy Skills Imperial Prosperity," *Globe & Mail*, December 7, 1995.

"Why E-mail is Dangerous," *Forbes*, July 27, 1998, p. 94.

"[Neil] Postman Delivers Warning about High-Tech Teaching" *Globe & Mail*, March 14, 1996: p. C1–C2.

3 How Mistakes Occur: The Seven Deadly Sins of Decision Making

"Those who cannot remember the past
are condemned to repeat it."
George Santayana, 1863–1952

So, just what does go on when all those highly paid executives and the managers who support them, sit down to make a decision? Do they accumulate studies, customized to their company's particular requirements, to inform their decision? Do they insist on the presentation of arguments both pro and con the decision at hand? Do they involve a wide range of knowledgeable advisors, both from inside and outside their organizations?

As any fly on the wall could tell you, multimillion dollar decisions affecting thousands of people are taken everyday by any method but the above. A great many business people, who should know better, commit one or more of the Seven Deadly Sins of decision making each and every day of their working lives. Whether they are spurred on by arrogance or greed, whether it stems from a fear of being seen as outdated or from a fear of hearing the truth, too many business decision makers fall into the traps outlined in Chapter 3 of this book. They either ignore available information which tells them their plans are doomed to fail or do not seek it in the first place, even though such information can often be found at modest cost relative to the decisions at hand.

Although each of these failings — or Seven Deadly Sins — is presented in a separate section, it is important to remember they are all interrelated.

Sometimes a poor decision is attributable to just one sin but more usually, decision makers are committing several sins simultaneously.

And what are some of the repercussions of this? Read on to learn about those who make ill-informed decisions, and who in a company is most likely to do so.

We Already Have All the Answers

The longer someone works in an industry, the more they are inclined to believe they know all the answers about that industry. And the more someone works for a particular company, the more they become immersed in that particular company's viewpoint. Out of this insularity is born one of the more common reasons people make the wrong decisions, a belief that: we already have all the answers.

Familiarity Breeds Contempt

This belief in the infallibility of a company and its point of view is particularly prevalent in large companies. Sheer size is deceptive; many managers and executives who work in multinational organizations with multiple locations are quickly and easily seduced into believing their company is the repository of all the knowledge they will ever need.

That this is not the case is shown in the example of what happened to the Big Three auto makers in the early 1970s, when Detroit automobile manufacturers were operating on the premise that they knew the market, knew what consumers wanted, and needed no "reality check." In the face of the oil crisis and the emergence of the Japanese car makers as a domestic threat, this thinking proved to be erroneous. Detroit did *not* have all the answers and went from being an unchallenged leader in the marketplace to playing catch-up as consumers switched to smaller, more fuel-efficient cars. It was only when the Big Three realized they did not have all the answers and set about finding them, along with making changes to their internal cultures, that they were able to rebound and regain some of their lost market position. But the world in which they operate had changed forever; in spite of any changes that they have made, non-Big Three competition is a way of life and the near-exclusive markets Detroit manufacturers once enjoyed will never return. All because they believed they had all the answers.

Going Outside for Information

Sometimes, this "we already have all the answers" syndrome manifests in the form of arrogance. Not simply content to rely on internal information, more than one manager at a large multinational has been heard to say, in response to outside suppliers of research services: We would *never* go outside for information! One can only speculate about the types of vacuums in which these people operate. *Never* go outside for information? Do these people not have customers and suppliers? Do they not have needs for products and services? Do they not attend conferences or participate in trade shows? It is virtually impossible for anyone to operate a business without going outside for information! Perhaps in some corporations, this stems from a fear, that admitting you may not know the answers is a weakness and that the organization must be perceived as self-sufficient in all areas.

"Old Boy's Knowledge"

These behaviors are particularly common in long-established companies operating in mature industries where there has historically been slow, if any, change. In such cases, this might be more appropriately referred to as "Old Boy's Knowledge" Syndrome, where executives, having served in the company and the industry for 20 or more years, believe that they know all the answers. This was definitely at work at an insurance company which suddenly found its market changing rapidly in the face of regulatory changes and other shifts to a more global economy. The front line workers, the people who tracked market segments and products, the sales force, those responsible for placing advertising and designing promotional campaigns, were fully in support of an outside supplier's competitive intelligence service, which supplied monthly reports of competitors' activities. But the service was axed by senior managers who firmly believed the service was a waste of money as they knew all the answers. Without the regular "reality check" which the report provided, the staff at lower echelons of the organization found it increasingly difficult to take the appropriate defensive measures to protect the company's market position. As external changes in the environment continued unabated, this company found its growth stalled and its market share challenged by new competitors as well as new forms of competition.

That going outside for information is a wise decision is shown by the example of the J.M. Schneider Corporation, a supplier of packaged meats.

Although the company was well-established in several U.S. markets, the concern had grown about why the company was in these markets. Volumes had driven such decisions in the past but now the company wanted to be more marketing driven. Yet, very little was known about the markets in which the volume accounts were located.

The company therefore set out to learn more about these markets, which included Western New York, upstate Florida, the mid-Atlantic state of North Carolina and other cities in and around these areas. A lot of the questions Schneider was asking involved demographics, neighborhoods, economic profiles and the business composition in each community. With this information, the company hoped to develop a better understanding of how many consumers fit an upscale profile, how future-oriented the companies were, what the long-term job market would be like. This would then suggest which markets were worth ongoing investments to develop more business and which markets should be slated for exits.

Given that the information was all readily available, all it took, for Schneider to make the right decisions, was the knowledge of where to find it and the time to put it together. As a result, the eventual decisions were wise ones, all because the company recognized that it didn't have all the answers.

History Does Not Always Repeat Itself

Companies which have been in business for some time and have, on the whole, been successful can fall into the "we already have all the answers" trap because their past track record of successes suggests they do. What they fail to realize is that the rate of change is accelerating; what did work well over the last 10 or 15 years may not hold as the market conditions which contributed to a stable environment disappear.

The railroad industry in the United States is an example of one where, for many years, rail for both freight and passenger travel was uncontested. Whatever tactics had been used to market and operate rail service, had been successful — in the past. But the emergence of new forms of mass transit, such as air, and the increasing pressures on businesses to deliver more and more quickly — as by air or road — changed the dynamics. Eventually, those running the railroads realized that past practices weren't a surefire recipe for success anymore and made changes, but not before there had been some financial casualties. In this case, the companies internally available information provided inadequate answers. What had worked in the past did not hold all the answers.

Even the presence of good internal sources of information, such as an in-house library or information center, can be deceptive and lead people into the folly of believing such resources "have all the answers." However clever the people running such centers and stocking them with information are, their powers of prognostication only go so far. No corporate librarian or information center manager can be expected to foresee *all* the information needs which could arise in the context of decision making. It is unreasonable to expect this of any human being.

But many is the business decision maker who allows the presence of such resources to act as a convenient excuse for only making a cursory examination of information to make a decision. The fact such in-house information may only be a starting point and should be fleshed out with recourse to additional and particularly external sources gets glossed over.

Question Migration

Such situations are fertile ground for companies to start practicing the question migration mentioned earlier. They look at available information, the "answers" they already have, perhaps from their internal information systems and start to kid themselves. "We really need to know imports for optoelectronic components" they say, but when government-compiled import data only reveal figures for 'Components, NEC' (Not Elsewhere Classified), such decision makers decide they'll make do.

The fact such data is needed to decide whether the company should continue to invest in R & D in such components or not, and that differences, in import figures, of a few hundred or thousand have a huge impact on whether such investments will be profitable or not, gets conveniently swept under the rug.

The Seeds of Future Strife

The business of the 21st century will only be able to indulge in believing it has all the answers at its own peril. When competitors may be investing increasingly in more and better information, any corporation which believes it already has all the answers will be the one most likely to be eclipsed as competition intensifies.

One only has to look at the pharmaceutical industry in the late 1990s to see how such current beliefs sabotage future success. Not only does the pharmaceutical industry believe it has all the answers for today, it believes this information, and the underlying worldview, will carry it through forever. Whenever the possibility of displacement from the rapidly growing alternative health field is mentioned, most pharmaceutical giants scoff at the notion. Herbal remedies? Homeopathic tinctures? Not a chance these will ever amount to much. The fact the consumer population is increasingly disenchanted with the drugs produced by the pharmaceutical companies is conveniently ignored. The fact a substantial amount of information, showing both the popularity and efficacy of these non-drug remedies is available, is of no interest to these companies. But ignoring this information is the underpinning of many decisions currently being made by pharmaceutical companies, which the next 10 to 25 years will show us to have been horrendously bad decisions.

Perhaps they are becoming less inclined nowadays to ignore information from another direction which points to decisions to be made in the not-so-distant future: the level of fatalities due to adverse drug reactions. This, combined with the growing evidence that "super bugs," resistant to many known medicines including antibiotics, are emerging, provides readily available information which should not be ignored by anyone in the drug industry making decisions today for tomorrow.

Entrepreneurial Errors

Small and medium-sized companies can also make the same error, but usually for slightly different reasons. Smaller companies are more prone to believing they have all the answers by practicing question migration and the usual reason they do this is because it allows avoidance of spending money (the role of money in decision making will be discussed later in more detail).

These are the folks who want to expand into new markets but, faced with new competition, rather than pay to find out about it, rely on 5-year-old articles or 2-year-old advertisements as a way of assessing how tough or otherwise the competitor is. Smaller companies are frequently tempted into rationalizing about the information they have — for expansions, purchases, acquisitions and the like — solely on the basis of what it would cost to investigate and find out for sure.

Who Are the Main Culprits?

Are all companies equally susceptible to committing this type of sin? As mentioned earlier, large corporations, the multinationals with thousands of employees, are particularly prone to making this mistake and need to guard against it. Some already do; among the global giants, some pharmaceutical companies are more receptive, than their peers by size in other industries to challenge their assumptions about current markets. Financial services companies are less likely to go outside but still realize they need the reality check from the marketplace to support much of their decision making.

Large manufacturing companies are perhaps more likely to commit this sin than their non-manufacturing peers while, as referenced above, small and medium companies usually in their rush to save money, commit this sin regularly.

At the individual or executive manager level, people who fall into this trap tend to do so more for reasons of corporate culture, especially if they work in an environment where the cultural norms stress self-sufficiency. Such corporate cultures may also be those which practice a type of paranoid secrecy — rather than just a prudent secrecy — neither sharing nor seeking out information.

What is the Cost of this Kind of Decision Making?

In the case of the Detroit automobile manufacturers, who believed they had all the answers, the cost of committing this Deadly Sin can be measured in their financial performance; year-to-year sales declines, at the corporate level as well as in the drop in earnings for their dealers. Chrysler alone posted losses of $52 million in 1974. It can also be measured in terms of the per-hourly increases unions were, or more accurately weren't, able to negotiate for their members. (Of course, in a case like this, one organization's loss is another's gain; a pick-up in results for the Japanese and other foreign car manufacturers created an offset for the economy as a whole).

As for the insurance company discussed, the cost of believing it had all the answers can be measured in underwriting business lost to new competitors, again, in the multimillions, particularly new direct writers which entered a market the company had pretty much had to itself in the past.

But for a company like J. M. Schneider, which realized it did not have all the answers, any costs, from market withdrawals, could be contained and limited to the short-term, because the company had a much better compass to the future.

Asking the Wrong Questions

Getting to the right decisions means having the right information. And getting the right information means asking the right questions. And here lies the nub of another reason why many business people make the wrong decisions: they do not ask the right questions.

The business archives of recent years are littered with many examples of how companies which do not ask the right questions end up on the wrong path. The example of Canadian Tire, an automotive and hardware retailer, which expanded into Texas a few years ago, demonstrates how the wrong questions can sabotage a business venture.

Texas was selected as a market by this company for expansion on the basis of the state's reliance on the automobile. The questions asked to form the foundation of the expansion decision included: How many cars are there in Texas? How far do people have to drive to work? What are the alternatives to self-driving, such as public transportation? The answers to these and similar questions indicated a large, automobile-dependent population, with — the assumption went — extensive, ongoing needs for automobile accessories, replacement parts, and related supplies, such as oils. Canadian Tire therefore bought an existing chain in Texas and began to operate this as it did its stores at home.

A success story in embryo? Hardly. By the time the Canadian retailer sold its operations in Texas, it had lost millions. Furthermore, this failed expansion led to the ouster of the long-time president who heretofore could do no wrong.

Unasked Questions

What led to this sorry state of affairs was the questions the retailer didn't ask before the purchase was made, such as: What is the reputation of the company we are buying? Who shops there and how often? Have sales been going up or down? Why? If down, can we reverse this trend? How is the Texas automotive aftermarket different from the Canadian? What is competition like? And how accepting are Texans of outsiders?

It was the lack of asking these last two questions in particular which really proved to be their undoing. The level of competition and hostility to those from elsewhere put this company at a huge disadvantage from day one, minute one. Since they had not foreseen this and had no strategy for dealing with it, all their other efforts were doomed. And why were only the "wrong" questions asked? (Actually the questions which were asked weren't wrong in and of themselves, it's just that they were wrong in isolation from other questions which should have been asked). Simply put, the questions which were asked were the ones which could be answered easily and cheaply from readily accessible sources of information. Statistics about cars on the road, commuting distances, public transit, etc. are all in the public domain. The unasked questions were those which would have required in-depth, original research, all of which costs money (an issue we'll look at in the section "Flying by the Seat of Your Pants").

Interestingly enough, this same retailer ended up in a similar situation when they expanded into the Chicagoland market a few years later. When a research supplier contacted them early on, offering expert research services, the executive in charge said: "Oh, our people down there know what they're doing." The assistance was declined; within three years, the retailer had to pull out of the market.

Unanswered Questions

Since none of the pitfalls in decision making covered in this book really exist in isolation from one another, it is easy to see a pattern here, in that companies which believe they already have all the answers are no doubt equally susceptible to asking the wrong questions when taking initiatives, such as expansion, outside their domestic markets. Whether it is mainly very large organizations with deep pockets which are most susceptible to falling into this trap or not is beyond the scope of this book but similar patterns can be found in the example of Toy's 'R' Us and its children's clothing arm, Kid's 'R' Us, when the company tried expanding into the Puerto Rican market.

Lured by encouraging birth rates and the rate of family formation in Puerto Rico and observing that other retailers from the U.S. mainland, such as JCPenney, had gone into Puerto Rico, seemingly successfully, Toy's 'R' Us decided to expand. Within a year, facing mounting losses, the organization had to pull out, leaving a textbook example of how asking the wrong questions or not asking any questions to begin with can jeopardize even the most well-funded enterprise. Much of the retailers' game plan had rested on the premise of back-to-school sales, long a staple of the children's wear and school supplies markets in the U.S. Most retailers based in the 48 states can count on a sizeable upswing in sales in mid-to-late August and early September, as parents get their kids kitted-out for school. Why did this not happen in Puerto Rico? Simply put, children there wear school uniforms and so there is no need for parents to buy a lot of clothing for the new school year each fall. Why a large, well-funded organization could not find this out — all it would have taken is the cost of a plane fare or two, to fly some decision makers down there to look things over — is not the point; the story illustrates how formulating the right questions at the start of any business initiative and obtaining the right information is crucial to success.

One Key Question is All it Takes

This fate was avoided by a company in the office coffee services business when it was in the process of expanding into the United States from Canada. On the acquisition trail, the company had identified several states where rapid population growth and business formation suggested the territory was fertile for them to acquire an existing supplier. The outside research firm they hired to identify prospects was armed with a list of questions, including questions about ownership — which companies were still privately held and where the owner was perhaps looking to retire — questions about the customer base and about business profitability. However, when it came to the state of Utah, one of the target states, the research company encountered a unique reaction from people interviewed. Even though the objectives of the research had not been mentioned, office coffee services operators in that state were begging: Please, buy my business! Further investigation revealed that Mormons aren't supposed to drink coffee and in spite of rapid population growth in the state of Utah, the prospects for any office coffee service business were limited. This turned out to be a pivotal question and the information supplied to the company on the acquisition trail was enough to have them strike Utah from their list of prospect states and concentrate their efforts on more profitable areas, such as North Carolina. Had the question not been asked and the information not uncovered, their fate could be the same as the hardware retailer and the children's clothing chain, an unprofitable initiative based on poor or no information.

Where the Wrong Questions Lead

The legacy of asking the wrong questions, over a period of time, can perhaps be illustrated by the predicament in which McDonald's found itself by the late 1990s. Once the undisputed leader in the fast food segment, the company was experiencing slowing growth and increasing problems in its domestic market, in spite of a still sizeable market share. Other fast-food restaurants, notably Wendy's and Burger King, seemed to be doing better in anticipating customer tastes and needs.

The causes of McDonald's predicament were reckoned, by analysts, to be many faceted, one being a failure to remain relevant to U.S. culture. Another reason was a failure to adapt the menu to new tastes. Whatever the reasons, the sad fact is: the information, to avoid these problems, has been readily available all along. If a lack of relevance is an issue, then the demographic data describing the changing face of the American population have been there all along. Shifts in ethnic composition, in socioeconomic status, in lifestyle segmentation have been available and accumulating for 20 or more years before their impact was felt.

Changes in dietary preference, including consumer desires for more natural foods, concerns over ingredients and food preparation methods or a simple inability to digest heavy meat meals (a characteristic of an aging population with declining levels of stomach acid) could have been spotted, coming over the horizon, long before such trends had an effect on the company. Such information is in the public domain and is well known. You just need to ask the right questions of the right people: the nutritionists, alternative health care practitioners, customers and others.

Another industry which will fall prey, sometime in the 21st century, to having asked the wrong questions in the 20th, is the tobacco industry. Much of the attention of the tobacco companies has been on the regulatory and legal climate in which they operate. Those not so occupied seem more concerned about competitors' new brands and test marketing initiatives, issues that have a three month to six month horizon. Had such people bothered to look to the broader environment, they would have seen signs indicating even bigger trouble on the horizon. The use of tobacco for medicinal and nutritional products is just one example; patents being filed in the 1990s indicate there could be an entirely different market for the tobacco crop by the second decade of the 21st century. Cigarette manufacturers currently operate on the assumption they will be the only purchasers of the crop; what if there are competing interests, especially more wholesome, socially-acceptable interests? What would this do to prices and therefore costs? But tobacco manufacturers were too busy asking the wrong questions, about immediate competitive product or class action lawsuits, to ask the right questions for longer term profitability.

Too Few Questions Can be Troublesome, Too

Not asking enough questions can also derail decision making as much as the wrong ones. A few years ago, the U.K. arm of Lawson Mardon, the packaging company, was seeking acquisitions in the eastern part of the United States. Target companies were to be involved in print lamination with revenues of $175,000 to $350,000 and privately held. The director responsible for the acquisition program, having delivered this mandate — which was to be executed over a 1 week timeframe — then went on the road and could not be reached.

As soon as the search for information began, further questions began to surface. Did print lamination include paper-based stocks and plastic? How about polyethylene coated papers? Hot mylar laminations? Were companies laminating counter cards, menus and p-o-p displays of interest? What about automotive applications? Or adhesive coatings?

Given that the director had considerable hands-on experience in the printing industry and knew exactly what sort of company Lawson Mardon was looking for, the initial questions provided, being too few in number given the importance of the acquisitions program led to a list of companies being developed many of which were not really of interest. As a result, the initial investment in list development was not well placed while the acquisition program was delayed to allow for better refinement of the list.

Even expansion closer to home can prove problematic. Pepsi Cola Canada, in 1996, had successfully launched a six pack of 710-ml fully resealable bottles bound together by a plastic ring in Quebec, to consumer response levels which achieved higher rates than any other brand launch by the company since 1984. But in neighboring Ontario, the product, instead of meeting with enthusiasm, drew the ire of both environmentalists and municipal officials. Part of the problem stemmed from the advertising campaign which stated: What a dozen cans look like when they're easy to carry, alongside a picture of the six bottles.

The merest suggestion that soft drink companies might abandon the aluminum can is a big threat in a province where laws oblige the municipalities to operate curbside recycling programs. The return on recycled aluminum is much higher than the return on recycled PET, meaning aluminum recycling helps defray the costs of the recycling programs, which currently are money-losers.

Had Pepsi-Cola asked a few more questions about the environment in Ontario or likely obstacles to the product, it might have avoided controversy by running a different ad campaign or simply by not introducing the product in the first place.

Backtrack When Necessary

Asking the wrong questions is not such a sin if a company is willing to recognize the mistake, backtrack and then go forward with the right information and the right decisions.

This was what Tyson Foods had to do when it initially launched a new roasted chicken product in the late 1980s. Most of the questions asked to support introduction of the product had been directed at individual consumers or end-users. There was a definite need for pre-cooked convenience foods that the roasted chicken met.

What Tyson Foods neglected to do was ask its trade customers, the supermarkets and food stores, about their needs. (Not surprising; many manufacturers or producers of consumer products sold at retail forget they have two sets of customers: their distribution channel and the end-user).

Turns out that there were problems, at the supermarket level with shelf life and how the roasted chicken fit in with existing inventory practices. The solution was found when information about these concerns surfaced and Tyson Foods began to pay more attention to their distribution channel.

Rather than write the roasted chicken product off (since it had test-marketed well), which is what some companies would have done, Tyson Foods recognized it had asked the wrong questions at the start of the exercise; by backtracking and then moving forward, the situation turned into a winner.

Who are the Main Culprits?

While some of the Seven Deadly Sins may be committed in a pattern characterized by type of industry, asking the wrong questions is more often the sin of those at a particular point of development; namely, among companies in an expansionary mode, whether at home or abroad. Perhaps this is attributable to the fact expansion tends to require deep pockets and, as discussed earlier in this book, abundance breeds indifference? Such companies can often easily afford the investment in information so that their decisions can be shaped to be the right one, so a lack of financial resources is not the reason.

Rather it is a question of buoyancy and naive self-belief. Things have been going well, growth in the original market or location has been in the double digits (or higher), the company can obviously do no wrong, and so off they go. Ironically, such initial expansionary outings, buoyed as they are by such confidence, are often the company's first experience with making a bad decision. This leaves them "licking their wounds" and more inclined to be cautious next time.

While expansion overseas may be the way large companies commit this sin, they can equally do so by buying new facilities or having them built from scratch. More than one company has believed its great growth will go on forever and then found itself mortgaged to the hilt, the proud possessor of several million square feet of space it does not need.

Asking the wrong questions, for smaller companies, tends to show up closer to home. The operator of a single store, restaurant or hair salon, rather than being content with the "goose that laid the golden egg" they already have, decides they need a chain. The questions such operators fail to ask are many and varied but one obvious one is: Do I have both the physical stamina plus the management ability to run more than one location? Except for misanthropes who really want to get rid of their social life, the truthful answer to this question is: No! But many ambitious entrepreneurs fail to ask it.

What is the Cost of this Kind of Decision Making?

Studying the annual reports of publicly traded companies recently withdrawn from the expansion trail will usually produce discreetly worded references to "one-time costs" or "write downs" or other allusions to their folly they hope no one will notice. The dollar sums are often far from reticent: hundreds of thousands all the way up to several million.

Even when the culprit is a large, multibillion dollar concern which can absorb the cost, the question still remains: What else might have been done with the money? What development of existing markets or products, or training of people might have yielded a better return? In such situations, the real cost goes beyond money spent on the experiment and shows up in its effect on the ongoing operations, sometimes to the point of crippling these.

And, among the entrepreneurial classes, the impact can be more severe. Not only may the original 'license to print money' fail, as the owner's attention is diverted, but this individual may lose life-savings, their home, their car, investments plus end up in debt. A high price to pay — but this is the legacy of asking the wrong questions.

Old Demon Ego

The reasons business people make the wrong decisions often stem from a multiplicity of causes; a belief in the infallibility of your own information and asking the wrong questions are just two of them. Whereas once mothers were concerned that their sons would go off and become enslaved to the "Old Demon Rum", a better piece of advice, today, to their sons — and daughters — would be to avoid enslavement to that other saboteur of good decision making: "Old Demon Ego."

More than one company has been brought down by this type of decision making at the board or executive committee level. The downfall of RJR Nabisco, to cite one example well-documented elsewhere, cannot be divorced from the egos which fueled the leveraged buyout, spurred on by greed. A refusal to look at available information, which indicated the course of action was unwise, was compounded by this demon at work.

Have You Hugged Your Pet Idea Today?

Decisions which companies should never take, and would never take if egos could be set aside, do get taken because decision makers can't give up their pet ideas. What is most tragic in these cases, especially for the people negatively affected in terms of layoffs and lost career opportunities, is that the decision makers often know they should go and get some objective input to test their idea but they deliberately avoid doing so. That's because they know an input of information will likely show up the flaws in the pet project. That would mean they would have to abandon the idea. The fact that hanging on to and following through on a bad idea will often have million dollar repercussions down the road gets pushed to the back of the decision makers' minds.

Old Demon Ego was certainly at work at a trust company which planned to introduce a new structured investment or "passive management" product to Canadian pension-plan sponsors. While widely accepted in the U.S. and the U.K., passive management was new to the Canadian market. Research was undertaken to determine receptivity and over and over, the answer came back the same: people just weren't interested. But the vice president of the division overruled this feedback and plans went ahead.

Two years later, as he was sitting in an office with a lot of empty desks and chairs around him, he had to admit the research had been right. "I should have listened to you," he told the research company, "but I thought I could overcome the negatives." By this point, his staff had all quit, taking to other firms the few clients who had been signed up, and he was on his way to another job, first inside his company but, within a few months, at an entirely different firm.

Unwise Acquisitions

As mentioned above, Old Demon Ego is frequently responsible for failed acquisitions and mergers. When a company sets out on the acquisition trail it is not always as the result of well thought out strategy. Many such purchases may as well be referred to as "trophy acquisitions" which address a lot of ego needs among decision makers but don't make much sense from a financial or business point of view. It takes a huge amount of rationalization for a steel company to diversify into silicon chips or for a distiller to launch into sound recordings; no wonder, then, that information is not obtained to test the idea in the cold hard light of reality. The ego-driven decision maker knows that such pet projects would never stand up to scrutiny.

Diversification Bites

Business diversification can equally fall prey to Old Demon Ego decision making. And companies, which should know better, are susceptible to being led astray this way. A large, highly successful company, a maker of soaps and detergents and the very model of a modern consumer goods organization, a few years ago decided it needed to diversify. And one of the industries selected for this was: dental supplies. Since the company also made toothpaste and similar products, this was not quite such a dramatic departure but, given that toothpaste is sold to consumers and dental supplies to dentists, there were no strong parallels between the two businesses.

The company, to give it its due, did decide to research the dental supplies industry, particularly to find out about pricing for the product it was initially aiming to produce: drill bits. Those charged with handling the research set to work. Articles from the professional journals were sourced; product literature from existing industry players was obtained, interviews were conducted with sales reps. One researcher even flew to attend the major industry trade show although he found the large screen videos of root canal procedures and other visuals on display a little hard to take on an empty stomach first thing in the morning!

In short, no stone was left unturned in the search for information which all quickly pointed to one key fact: no-one was making money with drill bits. In fact, most dental supplies companies viewed these as loss leaders, almost give-aways to attract the more substantial business from dentists for other supplies.

Now, most companies, armed with this information, would have reconsidered their plans but not this company or, at least, the individual charged with moving ahead into this area. Drill bits it was and drill bits it would be! How long it took for the venture to start and fail is not known, but suffice to say, the company today is not active in the industry and quietly retreated from any interests in dental supplies a couple of years after these events took place. As for the individual in the grip of Old Demon Ego when the decision to enter drill bits production was made? No longer with the company.

Failing Overseas

The reason so few companies succeed by expanding away from home in the face of the number who attempt it can also be laid at the door of Old Demon Ego. All it takes is for one company in an industry to decide to expand into, say, a China or a Thailand or some such place, and then many other companies in the industry decide to jump on the bandwagon and take the same steps. It suddenly becomes trendy, with otherwise conservative corporations being afraid of being left behind or being shown to be out of step with the times. Many of these ventures are not well thought out and the companies undertaking them do not really understand the full dimensions of what they are getting into. An example of this is in the textile industry, where companies decided to contract out a lot of garment manufacture overseas, but have since been slowly and steadily bringing some of this work back into the domestic U.S. market. The visible cost savings in hard dollars are often by no means enough to cover off the invisible, soft costs that running an enterprise thousands of miles from home, in different cultures, with different languages, entails. People make such decisions because they think they will look clever, allowing ego considerations to overrule the cold voice of reason.

Old Demon Ego can equally overtake decision makers who find their industries are increasingly global while they face competitors from other countries they know next to nothing about. A few years ago, a large chemical company was in the process of deciding whether to keep or divest its division active in the sulfuric acid technology business. The industry had shifted to where just four or five global companies comprised the industry, companies located in either North America or Europe.

In order to make a sound divestiture decision, the chemical company decided to find out more about the other players. How large were they? How well funded? How innovative? How truly global? Research was therefore commissioned to find the answers to these and other questions.

Once results were in, they showed the sulfuric acid technology division of this company was really only a bit player on the global scene. The other players had greater reach, more people, were better established in the customers' minds, had other lines of business which were more complementary with sulfuric acid technology and so on. Time to get out of the business, the executives decided, looking around for a purchaser. This is when the managers who were most actively responsible, on a day-to-day basis for the division, decided to buy it.

Although they knew the division was at a competitive disadvantage and that being successful in the business required deep pockets, they arranged a leveraged buy-out and took the company over themselves. How long the euphoria lasted is not known, but today, the company is owned by one of the other major players studied in the original research. By ignoring the obvious — the scale of the industry and its nature — the managers allowed ego to over-rule the facts and suffered the consequences.

Entrepreneurial Weakness

It is not just the decisions of large companies which are stalked by Old Demon Ego; smaller, entrepreneurial companies are particularly prone to being sabotaged by this type of decision making. Many is the entrepreneur who has 'bet the business' one time too many and become overextended, branching out into too many ventures, in too many markets, without adequate capital.

Even companies which are adequately capitalized can endanger their fiscal health by Old Demon Ego decisions. Consider the example of a large auto parts manufacturer — and a very successful one at that — which decided to expand into tennis racquets and tennis wear.

To anyone who has ever successfully diversified or expanded a business, the choice for the new venture will immediately raise some red flags. How similar are the auto parts and tennis industries? True, they both comprise products (as opposed to services) but there the similarities stop.

A Poor Serve

Auto parts are sold primarily to the automobile manufacturers, the OEMs, or Original Equipment Manufacturers, as they are known. Most auto parts suppliers have stable contracts with the OEMs; before the products are made, the sale has been pretty much guaranteed. Not so with tennis racquets and tennis wear. There is no pre-sale of production tennis racquets (as opposed to custom models) and, as for tennis wear, this is largely a fashion item, especially in the women's segment of the business.

Research was nevertheless commissioned to support the decision and some warning signals emerged. Tennis racquets were largely made at one or two factories in Taiwan and hardly anywhere else in the world. Different brand names were applied before marketing the product but there was otherwise little differentiation at the production level and, according to industry insiders, including those at associations and other bodies governing the sport, there was no room for any change to this practice.

The realities of the tennis-wear segment were even worse. Unless players belonged to clubs with strict rules, there was no requirement to wear items designated as tennis wear; any top and shorts will do. Even when players did belong to clubs with rules, they tended to be a small percentage of the tennis-playing population. Worse, tennis was a sport affected by the graying of the population; many players dropped out in their fifties, either giving up sports altogether or switching to golf. All tennis wear retailers told the same story: it just wasn't a hugely profitable line to be in.

So, what did the auto parts company decide to do, in the face of all these red flags? The company had, after all, been started by an immigrant who had made the right decisions to build up the firm and was still at the helm. Rather than abandon the idea, they ignored the information and went ahead — but not for long. Today, the company sticks "close to its knitting" in auto parts. But why this brief flirtation with tennis wear? Turns out that one of the owner's children was obsessed with tennis. For a while then, Old Demon Ego ruled the day.

Ignoring The Demon

Yet there are many examples where ignoring the whisperings of Old Demon Ego can lead to a healthier business, greater long-term profitability and other benefits.

Trying to be one of the "Big Boys," as any small boy who has tried it will tell you, is not without its hazards. You can get seriously hurt if you attempt initiatives for which you are not well equipped. In business, this sometimes means admitting you are not a major player and will never be able to profitably play in this league.

Such a decision was made by Spar Aerospace when the company realized it was able to build a satellite once every two years while the other players were building one once a month. Spar therefore made a decision to become a parts supplier, picking a "league" for itself where it can more comfortably play. Taking such a step meant ignoring the whisperings of Old Demon Ego, which would have urged the company to try and remain in the Big Leagues, at all costs.

Future Imperfect?

That Old Demon Ego decision making has an unpleasant impact in the here and now is easy to see, but how will this type of decision making affect business in the future?

Every company and every industry, once it achieves size and prominence, runs the risk of thinking this *status quo* will continue indefinitely. Many decisions taken or not taken rest on this assumption. In the case of many industries, listening to the voice of ego instead of reason, causes decision makers to ignore the "early warning signs" of change.

Take the case of the automobile industry, which predicates much of its decision making on continual and expanding purchasing of vehicles. Making such projections ignores some of the information readily available today, which points up some of the changes in the wind which will have a negative impact on demand for vehicles, at least in North America.

One trend is of course the imminent upswing in the number of retirees as the Baby Boom reaches retirement age. A sizeable chunk of the population just won't be needing to jump in the car and race off to work each day. What will this do to demand for automobiles, especially if those still working, the Generation Xers as they're known, can't afford or do not wish to buy vehicles (a trend which some have pointed to?)

Driving Off Into the Sunset?

Ah, yes, the auto makers will say, but all those retirees will need to drive out and about for recreation. But what if they can't drive? Many states and provinces in North America, for example, have age-mandatory driver retesting. What if this population bulge, in their 70s and 80s, starts failing their retest? (Apart from the fact there would be a sharp surge in demand for public transportation, the future would not be too bright for the automobile manufacturers unless they switched to building buses of various sizes). And, even if the Baby Boomers can pass their retests, what if health problems, such as degenerating eyesight, restrict or prevent them from driving?

Constant, neverending expansion in demand? Not very likely. And the developing world doesn't offer the hope some might contend it does; population levels, congested cities and lousy roads conspire to make these markets less than ideal, conditions which will continue well into the early part of the next century. (Not seeing what the roads really look like isn't just hazardous to auto makers with big dreams; a stockbroker, promoting Harley Davidson stock, opined that the growth outlook for the company was tremendous, because of the rapidly emerging markets in Asia. Hordes of the newly wealthy would surely be itching to buy a "hog." Anyone who has seen the crowded bazaars and pot-holed highways in some of these emerging markets will have trouble picturing anyone roaring off on a Harley!)

But unless some business decision makers take note of some of this information readily available today, the future will be less than perfect for the employees, customers and shareholders of such enterprises.

Who Are The Main Culprits?

Decision making which is spurred by Old Demon Ego, rather than being native to specific industries or an attribute of a company's developmental stage, is the presence of a certain type of individual. Anyone who bows to ego in how they make decisions is likely egotistical in many areas of their life: how they treat their staff, how they relate to their spouse, how they conduct themselves with their peers, how they deal with suppliers, in both their professional and personal lives. And, while both men and women can commit this decision making sin it, more than the other six referenced, does show a tendency to being gender-specific: men are much more likely to take gambles spurred on by the Demon.

Narrowing this down further, such decision making is more likely to rule the day at companies, both large and small, where the company founder is still at the helm. The example of the auto parts entrepreneur humoring the whims of an offspring is only one example; in the computer industry, there is one company whose founder–CEO is legendary for this type of behavior, so much so that someone wrote a book about him entitled *The Difference Between God and Larry Ellison.* Among those who are "hired guns," it's probably a fair assessment to say many of them are frustrated entrepreneurs; they never did start their own businesses but feel the need to make their mark in some way. Such executives can rarely tolerate being questioned about anything, no matter how small.

What is the Cost of this Kind of Decision Making?

In addition to any obvious hard costs of Old Demon Ego decision making, such as monetary losses, there is a soft cost which rarely is fully assessed: The loss of talent from the company as people leave for other jobs.

This type of cost can start at the highest levels — musical chairs seems to be being played as over and over, the Number Two person quits in frustration at the behaviors of Number One — right down through the ranks, as promising middle managers or juniors also feel the need to move on. This, in turn, has a longer-term impact on the well-being of a company as some of the better brain capital, those with the better detective skills described in Chapter 1, move on, impairing the company's overall decision-making resource.

Flying-by-the-Seat-of-Your-Pants Saves Money — Doesn't It?

Even when business decision makers avoid the traps described in earlier chapters, they nearly all fall into this one: by not seeking out the information to support decision making, they "save" the company money.

The thinking goes something like this: researching a potential acquisition/a new product/a competitor's marketing initiatives/a market entry etc. will cost $20,000? $200,000? $2 million? Heck, they say to themselves, we can "save" the company this money. Think how good we'll look! So they do not undertake investigations nor commission research — especially objective research from outside parties — and chuckle all the way to the bank, for now.

A Penny Saved is a Penny Burned

It is amazing how swiftly such "savings" turn into costs of far greater magnitude than the dollars not spent. Twenty thousand dollars to check out a potential acquisition? That's nothing, compared to the $20 million in costs they get hit with over the next two to five years, as the purchase turns out to be a "lemon." Two hundred thousand dollars? A mere pittance against the $200 million dollars worth of severance pay they have to fork over when an expansion sours and they have to lay off hundreds of people. Two million dollars? A drop in the ocean compared with $2 billion of legal expenses, environmental clean-up charges, lost operating revenues and ongoing public relations costs when the faulty design of their plant causes a major catastrophe.

But the "fly-by-the-seat-of-your-pants" decision makers never want to look at these facts. Not spending money — not quite the same thing as saving money — is the goal. Gripped by this myopia, they plunge ahead with whatever plans they have. In this way, they share characteristics with decision makers who believe they have all the answers and with those ruled by "Old Demon Ego!" But whatever the root cause, the same danger is present: a wrong decision will be made.

Observation suggests that such "savings" sabotaged the efforts of many of the bagel companies referred to earlier, who galloped to set up nationwide chains of bagel stores. Why spend the money to invest in research to learn about the level of competition when obviously the industry is booming? By not factoring in all the other places people could buy bagels and looking at this product in a broader, cultural context, several bagel companies overestimated the profit potential in the market. It's likely they were victimized by that other saboteur of decision making, not asking the right questions. Where do people buy bagels now and where do they prefer to eat them? Will they change their habits? Is the current growth phenomenon linked to the bulge in the population known as the Baby Boom and what happens when we reach the Baby Bust era? Of course, if you don't do any research in the first place, in the interests of "saving" money, you do not ask any kind of questions, whether right or wrong.

Winging it Overseas

This "let's wing it" philosophy creates a rationalizer's paradise and nowhere is it more prevalent than among those companies planning to expand outside their national borders. Conventional wisdom holds that, when you first expand away from home, you do it very close to your own shores. But when Malaysia or Brazil are posting such strong growth, not only do some companies not bother to fly there to check things out, they fly on faith in terms of how they make their decisions in the first place. When Coca Cola decided to increase its market share in the United Kingdom, early results suggest that the company entered the market in a "fly by the seat of your pants" style. In determining how best to boost sales in England and increase market penetration, the company studied *other soft drink manufacturers* and looked at their sales. Other issues of the broader cultural context seem to have either been ignored or merely skimmed over. The problem is, in the U.K. market, the broader cultural context actually held the real source of competition, which is tea; rather than facing competition from other soft drinks, Coca Cola really faced competition from tea and, more importantly, the long-standing British tea drinking habit.

While there are likely fewer traditional English families these days, given the influx of immigrants to the British Isles, what goes on in a traditional British house indicates how entrenched tea is in their way of life. Starting the day with a cup of tea in bed is a familiar routine to many; English people often have "teas-maker" machines in the bedroom to support their habit. Then, many will have a cup of tea — or two or three — at breakfast. Mid-morning, when people break for "elevenses," many will have another tea (although coffee is a strong choice here too). Move on to the lunch hour and it is not uncommon for people to enjoy another "cuppa," followed by a mid-afternoon tea break, which is in turn followed by a meal named Tea, where another cup or two will be imbibed. Then it's on into the evening, where some people will likely have a cup before they retire for the night.

It is not hard to see why starting a cola habit might be difficult, but the real gist of this story is: information about the English tea habit is widely available. Just stop people in the street and ask them. Why decision makers at Coca Cola did not find this out early on in their plans — staying in a few English homes would have given them the insight for free — is something of a mystery.

The Check is Never Going to be in the Mail

Another area in which companies decide to fly by the seat of their pants at great cost occurs when companies decide to undertake direct marketing efforts. Substantial investments will be made in the product, the mailing materials, the selling proposition, staffing to receive the flood of orders expected, and to otherwise prepare for what is expected to be a quantum leap in the company's fortunes. Then, the company will decide to "save" on the list used in the direct marketing. Given the amount of direct mail overkill experienced in North America and increasingly in developed countries overseas, skimping on the list of prospects is a very dangerous game to play. But even wealthy companies, planning to market big ticket items, are not willing sometimes to invest $15 or $20 per record to obtain highly qualified prospects on their list. Or, in the case of one software company marketing Enterprise Resource Planning software to corporate America, they insisted on using their own database with only a minimal infusion of cash to update the listings. How much mail actually went to non-existent companies or people who have long since retired, is not known, because companies are very rarely frank about these sorts of misadventures. But it is not uncommon for companies to have what they believe to be lists of their key customers which, during routine phone verification, turn out to list a surprisingly high number of people who have passed away these several years.

Manna from Heaven

What is often lurking behind this special form of "decision making" is that old bug bear of human behavior, procrastination. Even highly paid and highly trained executives in some of the world's largest companies believe that if they just wait long enough the perfect information to support their decision making will miraculously land in their laps without so much as the investment of a single sou. This philosophy fails to acknowledge the nature of information and what actually constitutes information, which will be discussed in more depth in Chapter 4 of this book. Most *readily available* information is generalized and intended to inform in a general way; rarely is generalized information, which just about anyone can access, tailored enough to support business decision making, which has to occur in the context of a particular company's situation. Even two companies in the same industry, embarked on expansion into the same overseas market, will not need to ask identical questions nor obtain the same information to shape their plans. While there might be some overlap, a lot of what each company will need to know is based on its resources, its mandate with its customers, how it does business, etc.

Fools Rush In?

Even when saving money is not the primary motivator, companies still choose to fly by the seat of their pants far too quickly for the magnitude of the decisions they have to make. Consider the case of Hawker Siddeley, a long-established railcar manufacturer. As everyone knows, they're not building railways like they used to, at least not in North America. (And, for practical reasons, railcars are of a size which don't lend themselves to exporting to parts of the world which are still railway-dependent.) And, as everyone also knows, the North American population is growing older and developing more eyesight problems. Heck, this is a no-brainer. The company should diversify away from the railway business and into eyecare. This is how Hawker Siddeley came to be involved with Beacon Eye Care Centers in the U.S., a company which, as press headlines in late 1997 showed, had fared very poorly and was the subject of numerous takeover attempts by other eyecare businesses.

While the events which led to this state of affairs are complex, information — or, more correctly, the lack of information at key decision-points — certainly played a part. What information should have been gathered and could have been gathered?

First there is ample information about the psychological aspects of eye surgery or any patient practices involving the eye. Ophthalmological journals have long included discussions of how to prepare patients for eye procedures. While laser-based surgery may be less invasive than traditional practices, most candidates for such procedures still feel squeamish about having things come at or near their eyes. This suggests there are many hurdles for laser surgery to overcome before such a business takes off, if it ever does. Then, there is a sizeable body of professional literature reviewing competing procedures, both laser and non-laser-based. Whenever new technologies are developed simultaneously, there is always a chance one will be displaced by the other or by later technologies, even if they are based on the same underlying principle, such as the laser. The warning signs are often there well in advance.

Then, there was information available about the people and interests behind the competitors to Beacon Eye. A convergence of the right funding, brains and motivation at one particular company can be enough to put one or more other companies in the industry at a disadvantage.

Last, but not least, information could have been relatively inexpensively dug up and examined showing how different the eyecare and railcar businesses are as businesses. One caters strictly to individual consumers, the other mostly to organizational purchasers. One requires a lot of marketing hype, the other relatively little. One requires numerous locations, easily accessible by public transportation; for the other, this was not a factor. And so it goes; had such readily available information been gathered and taken into consideration, the leap of faith from railcars into eyecare might not have been made.

Leaving it too Late

A corollary to this fly by the seat of your pants decision making is the practice of allowing too little time to properly gather, synthesize and analyze information. Take the case of a laptop computer manufacturer who had a product launch date already set and then called a research company to conduct market research to see if there was a market for the new features being introduced.

This all took place a few years ago, before laptops became widely used and the manufacturer, Siemens, had incorporated data security and access control into its product. The only problem was, at that time, potential customers couldn't have cared less about such features. Here was a case of a product being ahead of its time; however, think how much better the manufacturer might have done had they known about customer awareness of such issues. They could have either delayed launching their product or, they could have used their lead time in the marketplace to develop customer awareness of this issue while positioning themselves as the sole solution. The information which told them where the customers were at was readily available for a modest investment and was no further away than a phone call or two.

Which Came First?

Flying By The Seat of Your Pants decision making sometimes shows up in a "Chicken or Egg" scenario or: which comes first? Getting the right information to support the decision sometimes rests on putting the parts of the decision in the right order. A consulting firm based in Mexico City, anxious to take advantage of NAFTA signed by the U.S., Canada and Mexico, decided to pick Toronto for establishment of an office. Questions this consulting firm raised — and they were all good questions — included: Who were the potential clients, their numbers, size, the nature of their business plus the competitors, how they were delivering their data, and who they served. However, the one question they didn't ask and should have asked first is: Why Toronto? On examination of the consultants' services, which involved providing trade and business consulting services on a liaison basis between Mexican businesses and Mexican banks, it became clear that the market in Toronto might be immature for this type of service. But the consultants had already made up their minds; Toronto it was. As a result, their business never quite got off the ground and left them looking for a new location in the U.S. where there was more market demand for their services.

Winging It In The Future

The Fly-by-the-Seat-of-Your-Pants decision makers are equally inclined to sabotage their companies' futures by ignoring information available today and what it indicates for their businesses in the years ahead. The beer industry is another which predicates its outlook on not only ongoing but increasing consumption of its product. Whether a beer company measures its success in cases, gallons or hectoliters, the assumption is that, tomorrow, the customers will always obligingly buy more. What the decision makers overlook is that, as much as the customers might want to buy, they might not be able to. And such a development has little to do with consumers' earnings.

The peak time for capturing a beer customer is after the individual in question reaches legal drinking age (people who drink before they are of age is a market segment the brewers pretend doesn't exist). So, as an individual hits 18, 19, or 21, depending on their domicile, the breweries gear up their marketing machine. This person is ripe for the plucking.

What the beer companies consistently overlook is that many of these prospective beer drinkers, now in their childhood, pre-teens or teens, are increasingly riddled with allergies due to over-use of antibiotics. Notable among these is candidiasis, a condition many people have but can't put a name to. Candidiasis is linked to an overgrowth of yeast and once you know you have it, you don't drink or eat foods which contribute to the condition. This includes products with sugars and yeasts. Candidiasis is a "silent epidemic" that was only beginning to be recognized as such in the late 20th century. As more and more younger people fall prey to this condition, the beer makers will see a further erosion of their new drinker market which, coupled with fall-off from the retirees (since older people don't drink beer as much) doesn't bode well. Another factor from the senior segment of the market is the increasing incidence of diabetes, said to be rising alarmingly, which either limits or prevents someone from drinking any alcoholic beverages.

The brewing companies have also ignored another key piece of information which impacts both the present and the future and that is: half the population is female. Their "Fly-by-the-Seat-of-Your-Pants" decision making, coupled with Old Boy's Knowledge, has prevented them from ever developing beer products which truly appeal to female drinkers. And finding these products wouldn't require huge investments of capital either; Belgium alone has over 300 kinds of beer, including those based on fruit flavors. Since female tastes tend to run to slightly sweeter flavors, some might suggest finding ways to expand the beer business in North America, is a no-brainer. As this book is hopefully demonstrating over and over again, the information to make better decisions is all out there. All it takes is the time and resources to retrieve it.

Who are the Main Culprits?

Much like Old Demon Ego decision making, discussed in the last chapter, fly-by-the-seat-of-your-pants decision making shows up in a wide range of industries and in companies of all sizes. It tends to be more characteristic of individuals than sectors of the economy.

Even then, there are characteristics of these individuals which go hand-in-hand with their decision-making style. And chief among these is procrastination; if companies seem to be prone to making decisions in this way, then chances are their decision makers are also those who put off filing their tax returns on time, forget birthdays and leave many other details of their personal and professional lives to the last minute.

Another characteristic may be an inability to plan, no matter how much time is available; such executives and managers simply cannot see beyond the here and now or envision what tomorrow might look like. They may also have trouble picking goals and/or identifying the steps necessary to reach such goals.

At the company level, there is often a tendency for companies which are not so flush with cash to engage in this type of decision making, although they can ill-afford the consequences of a bad decision. At the same time, the circumstances which led to a depletion of cash reserves may also mean making decisions about new opportunities for the company cannot be put off any longer. (But then, it was procrastination which led to the situation developing in the first place).

What is the Cost of this Style of Decision Making?

Being unwilling to invest in information to support decision making, especially on a pro-active basis, before it is really needed, generally bears a high price tag. And that is the longer term cost of missing out on opportunities, of not taking advantage of shifts in the industry, of overlooking new markets which emerge.

In the case of the Hawker Siddeley/Beacon Eye venture, the net loss, for 1997 alone, was $23.9 million, which represents rather steep tuition for business decision making.

Such companies, which erode their future profitability by leaving key decisions to the last minute or undertaking them on a Fly-by-the-Seat-of-Your-Pants basis, are often those who end up being bought out so that they cease to exist. When such buyouts result in locations being closed or rationalization of operations, people who had no role in the decision making end up losing their jobs, adding a further cost. All because a handful of decision makers wanted to "wing it."

All Aboard the Bandwagon: If It Works for Them It'll Work for Us

Another type of decision making which leads to the wrong decisions being made is decision making by proxy; rather than undertake soul searching to find the right choices, a company instead looks around at what others in its industry have done and simply mimics them.

This is often true with decisions about automation; Company A discovers that Company B has installed a client-server network or added new software, so Company A decides it will do the same thing. The fact Company B's operations may be very different to Company A's, even though they're in the same line of business, doesn't enter their thinking. Company B may have had a particular problem to solve which means the automation made sense. Company A, by mimicking this behavior, may actually increase its costs or reduce its productivity by adding similar equipment.

Of course, one of the attractions of "if it works for them it'll work for us" thinking is that decisions made this way tend to be low-cost as far as a visible outlay of dollars is concerned. There is no need to gather objective information or conduct research. By imitating what others do, there is no need to take an idea and test it in the context of your own company to see if there is a fit.

Copycat Decisions that Work

This is not to suggest that looking at what others do is wrong in its totality. Learning from other companies is a very valid undertaking, most notably when undertaken as benchmarking or best practices work. This occurred a few years ago when Coca Cola decided to study the operations and cost structures of a particularly competitive private label bottler. Since many variables in both companies' operations were the same, i.e., cost of inputs such as sugar and cans, cost of labor (since both were unionized shops), cost of real estate and taxes, etc., Coca Cola was interested in finding out what the differences were. One, of course, was the cost of advertising, which the private label bottler did not have to sustain; what wasn't apparent, until an investigation unearthed it, was the fact that the private label bottler saved substantially on distribution costs by having its customers come and pick up their orders rather than maintain a fleet of its own delivery vehicles. This information allowed Coca Cola to re-examine its own way of operating with a view to making improvements.

Mimicry as High Art

Such benchmarking or best practices work, which turns mimicry into a high art form, involves in-depth research, extensive analysis of the results and considerable budget outlays. Without these three elements, it is unlikely any benefit would be derived. A "copycat" practice falls down, when there is no real thought or investigation of the proposed decision but rather copying at the shallowest level. There is also a growing body of evidence which suggests such benchmarking — or its close cousin — best practices research, only benefits companies which are already in the top tier of their industry.

Some people might try and refute the charges of decision making by proxy. Isn't it true they might argue, that Burger King's whole business development strategy is based on simply following McDonald's and putting new locations across from or near to wherever McDonald's is? The answer to this is: yes and no. While it is true Burger King may locate near McDonald's, this is not the example of shallow, imitative behavior, which it appears to be on the surface.

Long before Burger King settled on this strategy, it first had to investigate and identify the behaviors of consumers and learn that business in the fast food industry can actually be increased by being close to a competitor. While decisions today about new locations can seemingly be made by just copying McDonald's, they are actually based on long-standing analysis and are not examples of simple mimicry.

Another example of where copying not only worked but was unavoidable is that of frequent flyer miles. Once one airline introduced such a plan, all had to follow suit. But most of the followers studied the leader as much as possible before making this commitment. Without such programs, they realized their own business growth would be limited. At the same time, the cost of entry into such programs was low, requiring no major capital investment.

Copycat Decisions that Don't Work

Ignoring the costs of mimicry is why a major newsprint manufacturer came unstuck by copying others in its industry. Everyone seemed to be adding new "machines" as they are called, large Fourdriniers and the like, which are used to turn out newsprint. The company therefore decided to jump on the bandwagon and invest in new machines, too. This naturally involved a substantial capital outlay. Later, the Executive Vice President of the company moaned to a visitor in his office: God, I wish someone had told us about all this recycling stuff before we invested in new machines!

It is hard to believe that a senior executive in a large company could have been kept in the dark, whether by the ministrations of junior staff or by his own ignorance, about the trend to recycling of newsprint. Here is a classic example of where information was readily and widely available but wasn't tapped; long before this company invested in its new machines, the recycling movement had been gathering momentum and achieving more and more prominence. There had been substantial press coverage about curbside recycling programs. The need to recycle was being taught in the schools. Associations devoted to reducing pollution and waste had sprung up and achieved prominence. As with so many decisions, the underlying factors at work sabotaging the outcomes stem from multiple causes. This company was undone partly by being a copycat, sort of corporate "Keeping Up with the Jones" along with a dash of Old Demon Ego.

The siren song of "If It Works For Them..." may have had a bearing on why the current owners of the Koo Koo Roo restaurant chain decided to get into the fast food business — and, the fact jumping on the bandwagon rarely works out, may have a bearing on why many of the company's plans have not come to fruition.

Back in 1988 to 1990, when the Koo Koo Roo story really begins, fast-food chicken was dominated by organizations such as Kentucky Fried Chicken or Denny's. Such chains were perceived, by Koo Koo Roo's owners, as serving a low-income demographic, leaving the higher-income demographic untapped. Experiences in the Los Angeles area suggested high-income earners were a ripe market for an upscale healthy chicken and vegetables concept. Plans for expansion in California as well as neighboring Nevada and as far east as New York, New Jersey and Florida were formulated.

Koo Koo Roo's subsequent history suggests that whatever is working for KFC and Denny's is not working for the Koo Koo Roo chain. What readily available information was either not tapped or ignored, information which might have resteered the company to more success?

One type of information is that about the chains which are successful with chicken, Denny's El Pollo Loco outlets, KFC's locations, etc. Perhaps chicken just appeals more strongly to a lower-income demographic and does so on a regular basis? The "void in the marketplace" which the current owners claimed they could fill, might well have been a real void because there is insufficient demand. A corollary exists here: If it doesn't work for them, it likely won't work for you either.

There is also plenty of material published in a range of public domain sources which suggests that while a majority of Americans are concerned about their health, the way they address this concern differs across the country. Food tastes can often be highly regionalized or even localized; what people perceive as healthy food in Southern California may not be perceived the same way in the Midwest or the Southeast.

Following the Fashions

Such "jumping on the bandwagon" can undo otherwise well-intentioned companies. A few years ago, market segmentation became the rage, as companies started to segment their customer bases, identify which segments — which might be types of business in a business-to-business environment or particular demographics in consumer markets — they were currently serving, so as to identify where more prospective customers might most readily be found.

Segmentation strategies also promised to make marketing more straightforward, producing better returns, as marketing campaigns and materials could be tailored to each segment.

All fine and dandy for businesses which are either marketing-driven or do not face other practical constraints in how they serve their customers. Market segmentation does not really apply to businesses where physical geography and geographic proximity of customers one to the other is a more important factor, as in businesses where route density is a major determinant of success. But this was exactly the mistake a major waste hauling company decided to make.

In the process of building databases to serve as a foundation for business development and sales efforts, the company became obsessed with segmenting its customer base and targeting new accounts accordingly. There were already a number of restaurants and auto body shops among the existing customers — so let's target more of those! We already serve electronics shops and meat-packing plants? Let's get more of those!

The fact that, in a business where you send a truck to empty dumpsters, it is much more profitable to sign up all the businesses in a single location, such as a strip mall or an industrial park, rather than have a route zig-zagging for miles between, for example, auto repair outlets, was pushed to the back of everyone's minds. Eventually, of course, the folly of this approach began to have an impact on profitability, so everyone agreed to turn back to the tried and true. Another case of, if it works for them, it might not work for us.

Safety in Numbers

Looking at any other business and figuring it must be easy to run is an equally hazardous course of action. Consider what might have happened to a milled products company, a producer of breads, crackers, pastas, and such products, if it had thought getting into shrimp aquaculture was such a "snap."

Armed with a mandate of diversification as a growth strategy, the company's business development team undertook research to learn more about shrimp aquaculture. They were already considering several locations in different parts of the world but, before purchasing any sites, decided to obtain some more facts. Two key thrusts to the research were market information and technology factors.

It was just as well that they did investigate. Although the demand for shrimp was strong, especially in the food services sector, the market was not without its fluctuations, depending as it did on consumer preferences and individuals' tastes which can and do change on a whim. But even more important, from a technology perspective, shrimp farming is a high-risk business. Get the land wrong, never mind the wind or the water, and your whole operation is doomed. This was the story told by operators whose businesses had failed and who had suffered multimillion dollar losses as a result.

The numbers which came back therefore provided a safety valve, telling the company considering shrimp aquaculture that this was no field of endeavor for copycats and that the barriers to entry were high. As a result, the company dropped some sites from its short-list and scaled back its plans, to allow for proceeding more cautiously.

Why is No One Else Doing This?

The hazards of assuming "what works for them will work for us" can also be illustrated by the foray into disposable diapers made by Johnson & Johnson a few years ago. For a company known for its baby powder and shampoo, this was not such a bad idea, on the surface. In fact, the synergies looked quite promising.

The realities of the marketplace dashed that promise. Disposable diapers are dominated, in North America, by two giant producers: Procter & Gamble and Kimberley-Clark. Although Johnson & Johnson poured hundreds of millions of dollars into its line of disposables, success remained elusive. Eventually, Johnson & Johnson had to reach a conclusion: they were not able to compete in this business.

Some might say: Nothing ventured, nothing gained. While this is true, it is better to make the venture calculated and to do this takes information.

What information — readily available — did Johnson & Johnson not take advantage of? One piece of information is the nature of the product, which is paper-based. Both the dominant diaper producers have their own mills along with the expertise to run them. Johnson & Johnson should possibly have invested more in assessing how many barriers to entry existed for any newcomer given the nature of the pulp business which tends to require large capital investment.

Another key piece of information, which the company should have had ready access to, is the customer life cycle relative to the product: small children usually only spend a couple of years in diapers before they are toilet-trained. This means there is no long-term need for the product; the opportunity to build customer loyalty is of short duration only, the length of the relationship equally small. The same cannot be said of Johnson & Johnson's then existing baby products; many adults make use of baby powder and shampoo.

All such information could have been obtained at relatively low cost if Johnson & Johnson didn't already own it; perhaps, in this case, given it already marketed baby products, the company also committed the sin of thinking it had all the answers?

Forget the Carbon Copy

How might companies making copycat decisions today run into trouble in the future? Again, the information is all around. Consider anyone deciding to open a new ski resort or launch into production of skiing equipment or machinery such as snowmobiles. Existing operators of such resorts or factories no doubt make it all look easy. But a number of indicators of trends and changes on the way suggest that even if it works for the others today, in the future it will not only not work for you but might stop working for them.

One key trend is global warming, a trend that not even the meteorological experts can agree on. Some say the explosion of Mount Pinatubo reversed 100 years of global warming; others say warming caused by environmental pollution continues unabated. Whatever is correct the fact is, in some once-wintry parts of the world, there is less snow.

Coupled with this are the other standard demographic trends, such as the aging of the population; skiing is not an older person's sport. Then, socio-economic upheaval means that many of the younger, target population may not have the means to ski; it isn't enough to look at the number of children and teens in the population, you also need to look at how many of them can afford to take up the sport. It's no wonder that, in the face of such trends, companies such as Bombardier, which has been very successful for years with its snowmobiles, have diversified into products for other terrains or mediums, such as the Sea-Doo, while ski resort operators are racing to turn their facilities into year-round destinations or attract convention business.

Who are the Main Culprits?

Are there industries or companies which have a greater tendency than others to commit the "If it Works for Them it'll Work for Us" kind of decision making? Absolutely! This sin is most usually made in mature industries where there are a limited number of people and everyone knows everyone else.

If the playing field were populated by hundreds of companies it would not be as easy to copy; for one thing, it would be harder to see what others are doing and for another, the more players there are, the more likely markets are still expanding.

In mature industries, where there are often as few as three players, market growth has often slowed, meaning companies tend to be more focused on cost reductions as a way of keeping profits up. At the same time, with so few players — and possibly a dearth of product innovation going on — it is easy for one company in the industry to deduce a fair bit about what the others are doing, even if they are not inclined to share. So, if one of the players suddenly drops their prices or is able to splurge on new equipment, the thinking quickly becomes: they must be on to something. We better do it too!

Industries, such as the ones in which Johnson & Johnson participates, are increasingly dominated by fewer but ever larger players. In the case of diapers, industry consolidation had already occurred, leaving a playing field with serious barriers to entry to anyone else. In the case of the newsprint company, such consolidation had already begun and continues to this day. In the fast food business, while there are several nationwide chains, the "banners" or company names are operated by a shrinking number of owners who have considerable expertise and clout. However tempting it might be for someone outside to look at these companies and say "piece of cake!", it is not true that what works for them will work for someone else too.

What is the Cost of this Style of Decision Making?

In the case of Johnson & Johnson's adventures in diaperland, the cost of getting the venture off the ground has been described as "hundreds of millions of dollars" while the eventual write-off clocked in at $60 million.

For the milled goods company eyeing shrimp aquaculture, the losses of one failed entrepreneur who contributed to the research ran around $12 million — and this was just from one site. Had the company plunged ahead with several sites, it could have easily sustained losses on a scale of $100 million+.

And in the case of Koo Koo Roo, the company is reported to never have had a quarterly profit, which speaks for itself. But whatever the eventual price tag, jumping on the bandwagon is a risky type of decision making, with any loss too high and completely avoidable.

Hear No Evil

Another way companies avoid making the right decision is by making sure they never hear anything unpleasant. So entrenched are the myths, so fearful are the decision makers of the cold hard light of day, that they operate in a cocoon. Anyone who dares to question the myths or bring in information allowing reality to pierce the cocoon, is ostracized.

Those who practice the "Hear No Evil" style of decision making, usually bear some resemblance to those who think they already have all the answers as well as those who fly by the seat of their pants. Hear no evil decision makers are often great practitioners of question migration; that way, they control the process and the outcomes so the information they receive tells them what they want to hear.

Large and small companies are practitioners of this type of decision making, but we usually only hear about the large ones when they get into trouble — the IBMs, Kodaks, Singers, etc. The smaller companies usually fade from the radar screen unnoticed.

Controlling the Outcomes

Ironically, companies who practice hear no evil decision making, unlike some others, do get outside information into their companies but they generally take care to work with those who will tell them what they want to hear and with methods which will produce fairly predictable outcomes, giving new meaning to the expression "structured surveys."

When such companies conduct customer surveys, they avoid asking questions which are too probing or too naked, relying on "fill-in-the-blanks" approaches. Such questions and the choices respondents are given are generally designed so that the answers look pleasant. Such companies also further ensure they like the information they receive by speaking only with their existing customers and not bothering to survey their lost customers. The same is true of the market surveys they conduct; they survey their success in areas where they are strong and avoid conducting surveys in markets where they are weak.

A further tactic used by hear no evil decision makers is to work with outside consultants who will obligingly tell them only what they want to hear. Since there is always a temptation among consulting firms, if the fees are large enough and frequent enough, to compromise the integrity of research results and put a spin on findings to keep the client happy, Hear No Evil companies can go for quite some period of time without ever learning the truth about how they are doing or what is going on in their markets. The advent of fancy presentation graphics on desktop computers has gone a long way to contributing to hear no evil consulting; dressed up in pie charts and three-dimensional bar graphs, the truth can be easily hidden if not buried altogether.

Don't Tell Me What I Ask to Hear!

Even when such companies select consultants they are not familiar with, they are rarely weaned away from their preference of hearing no evil. A company in the sign business, which created neon and similar outdoor signage for organizations, decided to undertake an analysis of its competitors' finances and operations. The only trouble was, of the 20 or so target companies, nearly all were privately held and the sign manufacturer had no data. A research company was therefore called in and charged with building profiles of each of the competitors.

All of which was duly completed and presented to the client. As the research company explained, the sources used were varied: filings with government, such as leased property records; credit reports; articles and product literature; plus calls to a range of contacts at each company, including financial officers, sales reps. and production people. The resulting financial data — which sometimes had to be phrased as a range — was based on the cumulative effect of this background material.

The sign manufacturer's president wasn't buying any of it. "I *know* this company doesn't make this much," he exclaimed, pointing to one profile. "I know these people don't make as much as this," he said pointing to another. And so on, down the list of companies. In fact, he seemed highly offended that any of his competitors would be making a sales figure greater than his. As far as he was concerned, his company was the biggest in the industry. That was the way he liked to think things were. It left the research company scratching its head and wondering to itself: In that case, why bother to ask someone to conduct research?

Very often, research from the real world *will* upset the "apple-cart of notions" which a company holds. Not finding out about reality, however, can skew decision making and put the company at a disadvantage. Perhaps that is really what the Hear No Evil companies want to achieve?

A Little "Evil" May be Good for the Corporate Soul

Those companies which do brace themselves to "hear some evil" tend to benefit in the long run, even if the message at the time is unpleasant.

Several years ago, when mainframe and mid-frame (or mini-) computers were still the choice of many companies, Prime Computer, a leader in mini-computers, had some research conducted in specific institutional markets which were key to the company, such as education and government. The objective was to find out satisfaction levels among the established customer base with Prime's delivery and after-sales service.

While information about both satisfied and disgruntled companies was obtained, the more valuable piece of information came from a question which was almost tossed in as an after-thought: What were the plans of these customers with respect to UNIX-based workstations?

The results left many decision makers at the company thunder-struck: about 23% of long-term, signed up customers were planning to switch when their contracts with Prime expired while another 25% were leaning in this direction. Not exactly good news but as Prime was open to hearing such "evil", the company at least knew what was on the horizon and could take steps. The information was described, by one manager, as "useful information you can take action around."

Not being receptive to "bad news" can stall a company's growth plans indefinitely. A maker of jams and preserves was eyeing expansion into the U.S. market. Having reached saturation at home, this seemed like the only avenue open to achieve long-term growth and maintain profitability. Prior to launching a full-scale market entry, the company had done some test marketing and decided the J.M. Smucker Company was the major competition to be concerned about. The real snag, though, was that the new entrant seemed to have trouble matching or beating Smucker's prices. What then, were J.M. Smucker's costs, the executive vice president mused to an external research company? He further admitted in writing that his company knew very little about their opponent.

At the time, J.M. Smucker was privately held and still much of a family business. Information therefore had to be pieced together from different sources and teased out of various contacts. Some of the targets, such as hourly labor rates and per capita benefit costs were difficult to retrieve. Other data retrieval was complicated by the organization of the company; J.M. Smucker did not buy its fruit on the open market but had its own farms. Obtaining costs of such inputs involved fairly detailed work. Learning about Smucker's label and bottle costs was also difficult.

A reasonable amount of detail was nevertheless presented to the jam maker. And the assessment? We already knew all this! exclaimed the vice president, while the company went on to withhold final payment to the research company. The real reason the work drew such ire? In the final analysis, Smucker had higher costs than the would-be market entrant but still managed to be more profitable. Not pleasant news, especially to another closely held family organization, which the jam maker was, one where, very rarely, the harsh light of reality was allowed to shine.

Shoot the Messenger

Being receptive to bad news and adjusting decision making accordingly is something however, that many companies are not. Most of the Hear No Evil school of decision making are equally likely to be practitioners of "Shoot the Messenger", especially when the messenger is an external research supplier.

This was certainly true of an insurance specialist who worked exclusively in the area of disability and buy-out insurance for high net worth entrepreneurs. He decided to have a research company develop a list of prospects for him, build a database in fact, with data about the companies — two or more partners, the current disability package in place, if any, when the contract expired and compensation of at least $150,000 per partner per annum.

The research company didn't have too much trouble finding prospective partnerships except for one small snag: those companies where the partners met the compensation requirements had no interest in any new relationship with an alternate insurance specialist. Or, they had reached the point where they could self-insure. Where there was a need — and a large untapped market — was among the businesses where the partners earned $75,000–125,000 a year. Could the specialist not re-design his product? the research company suggested. Was there no way to tap this market?

The insurance specialist remained adamant: $150,000+ it was and $150,000+ it had to be! The research company redoubled its efforts to find these "elusive butterflies" but the answers kept coming back the same: there was far less business potential in this market segment.

In the end, relations broke down, as the research company was accused of ignoring the directives and sundry other failings. But what was really going on is that the insurance specialist didn't like the message and couldn't adapt to market realities. Instead, he decided to "Shoot the Messenger."

Large companies also indulge in this practice when the decisions they want to make are shown by external information to be the wrong ones or that the corporation needs to re-think some of its myths.

A nationwide grocery wholesaler was facing a challenge from an independent, employee-owned wholesaler in one of its regional markets. Like the national group, the smaller organization also had both wholesale operations and retail stores. Its stores were smaller in square footage terms compared with those owned by the national outfit, but, industry scuttlebutt suggested they were much more profitable. What the larger wholesaler was interested in doing was finding enough information to be able to lower its own costs or make other changes, such as in headcounts, to compete more effectively.

Outside research counsel was therefore engaged to retrieve a range of data; size of the competitors' warehouses, amount of space devoted to dry goods and frozen foods, shifts per day, workers per shift, hours worked and productivity per worker. Details about number of trucks, truck bays, delivery routes and distances between the warehouse and the loading dock were also required.

This information was duly pulled together; the research company also visited the stores, noted layouts and square footages and thoroughly assessed the competitor. But along with the facts, the research report also contained this observation: the target company is employee-owned.

The national wholesaler, once in possession of the report, quickly let it be known that the information produced was decidedly "evil." The executive in charge grudgingly acknowledged that, if they could only get their employees to think like owners, things could be a lot better. But faced with a union, and an unwillingness to look too closely at employee share ownership, the wholesaler was at a stalemate.

Even to this day, the company has not been able to make fundamental changes nor adopt the better ideas of its nimbler, smaller competitors. Stores run by this company keep getting bigger and bigger — although the competitive evidence suggests smaller might be better — while head office relocation to lower and then still lower cost regions seems to be the norm.

Ironically, this company seems to be ignoring other, readily available information; the aging of the population. There is no guarantee an increasing number of older shoppers will be willing to walk the "miles of aisles" this company's stores now feature.

Misreading the Future

Ignoring information readily available today threatens the future of more than one industry. One that seems especially stubborn in this regard is the newsprint business; ignoring newsprint recycling, as already discussed, is just one manifestation of this. There are two other trends for which plenty of signs exist today.

One of those is the increasing trend to illiteracy or only functional literacy, at best, in the developed world. The repercussions from low-literacy levels stretch beyond even one industry but the potential impact on newspaper sales, threatens to be immediate (some claim it has already begun). But the various newsprint producers have their sights set firmly on the supply of trees, the grades of paper needed by newspaper publishers, the number of pages per paper and similar issues. In their day-to-day operations, few news-print companies seem inclined to address this slowly growing phenomenon nor look at how to address it.

The other issue many have either ignored or left aside for consideration another day, is that of alternative media, such as CD-ROM or the Internet. The fact such media could continue to erode the market for newspaper sales, doesn't seem to be as firmly on the agenda at some newsprint producers as it should be. But the information is all there; instead of ignoring it, such companies would do better to examine it and see how they can take advantage of the trends.

Who are the Main Culprits?

While companies both large and small can commit the sin of "Hear No Evil," it is much more likely to be practiced in organizations which are — or are fast becoming — shadows of their former selves.

Companies which were once the darlings of the industry but have lost some of their luster may have trouble facing up to the new realities. Dominant players who are being eclipsed by new entrants or young upstarts may, instead of finding out what they are doing wrong, find ways to hear only what they want to hear.

Family-owned or family-managed businesses are equally vulnerable to committing the Hear No Evil sin, especially when they are run by the third or fourth generation of the family and have been institutions in their industry for years. Such family-run enterprise is also likely to commit another deadly sin: Flying-by-the-Seat-of-the-Pants to save money.

And if anyone — usually an outside supplier because insiders may be too nervous for their jobs to tell the truth — has the temerity to bring the cold light of day into the company, well, then they Shoot the Messenger.

What is the Cost of this Style of Decision Making?

As with the other six Deadly Sins of decision making, the price tag on this one can become quite steep. Any company which ignores the "wake-up call" for long enough soon goes under or becomes a target for an acquirer. Anyone who has invested in such an enterprise, such as external shareholders, also suffers, indicating a further cost, thanks to those who Hear No Evil.

In the case of the shareholders of many newsprint companies, this might have produced some benefits in the short-term, if the acquirer companies make generous enough offers to those who hold stock in the takeover targets. But in the long term, the eroding demand for newsprint coupled with short-term fluctuations in demand, based on economic cyclicity, do not promise a healthy return. And for employees at these organizations, downsizings with their attendant career disruptions are an all-too-obvious cost to expect.

For a company like Prime, some of the costs associated with Hearing No Evil were actually avoided because the company could prepare defensive measures in the short-term. In the long-term, of course, the cost in any technology business, with its high level of displacement, will always be high.

And for the insurance specialist, the costs can not only be measured in lost opportunities — one which someone else would likely seize — but also in the cost of marketing a lost cause, covering operating costs and salaries while revenues stalled, and the general "spinning of wheels" which results.

Hurry Up and Wait: No Decision Can be the Same as a Bad Decision

As already mentioned, it is human nature to procrastinate and people who go into business are still heirs to this weakness of the flesh. Sometimes, when decisions and often major decisions have to be made in business, the decision makers procrastinate, and end up making no decision. As with most scenarios discussed, no factor works in isolation, and so this approach to decision making is a very close cousin of the flying by the seat of your pants to save money variety.

One of the unfortunate outcomes of taking no decision can be a lost opportunity. New product opportunities, not pursued, will never increase revenue. New markets, never entered, will never double the size of a business. New customers, never identified, will never buy from you.

If It Is Broke — Fix It!

Failure to make a decision doesn't just mean lost opportunity; it can also take away the chance to take corrective action to an existing business situation.

This was the case for a pharmaceutical manufacturer which made a product to treat perimenopausal problems. Long the dominant player, if not the only player in this category, the company kept putting off research into the various alternatives receiving approval, such as generics, along with ignoring the groundswell building in favor of alternative therapies and natural treatments. By refusing to take any decision about the future, these new market forces were like waves chipping away at a rock, eroding the manufacturer's market share. By the time the company sat up and took notice, the damage had been done. By procrastinating, the opportunity to take action and reverse the damage had long passed.

Another company which fell prey to the legacy of "hurrying up and waiting" was The Nutrasweet Company. Although the company was well aware of some of the competition emerging, so entrenched was the belief at the company about the importance of its aspartame product, that various market forces were ignored. There was also a tendency to believe that the customers would never dare switch to acesulfame-K or sucralose. As for alitame or products based on xylitol or lactitol, those were a joke! With its patents expired or expiring, and too few products in the R & D pipeline, the company was at a juncture where decisions should never have been avoided. Pointing out that there was also substantial work being done in natural sweeteners, such as abrusosides and steviosides, met with shrugs and disinterest. Suffice to say, The Nutrasweet Company no longer enjoys the exclusivity it once did while the market for artificial or non-sugar sweeteners has greatly expanded in terms of customer choice.

Even when companies are facing serious erosion of market share and need to do something urgently, they become practitioners *par excellence* of "Hurry-Up and Wait" decision making.

This was what a maker of office equipment did between July and December of one year. Years ago, the manufacturer's name had become eponymous with the type of equipment it made — much the way Kleenex is eponymous for a paper handkerchief — but by the late 1990s, a host of competitive product had taken away market share. What was going on, the manufacturer wondered, in its various retail and commercial markets? Why were distributors stocking the products they were? Which makes and models were the leaders? Information to answer these and other questions were required to formulate an action plan.

A proposal was therefore submitted by a research supplier in August. Then, the research company waited. And waited. In late September, the vice president called back. "Well, we think we pretty much know what's going on in our commercial markets. Revise the proposal to focus on retail." This was duly done, but it was only in October that the go-ahead was given.

Then, half-way through the research, the vice-president phoned again. "I don't know how far things have gone, but we pretty much know what the situation is with the office products retail distribution channels. Re-focus on other retail." This meant sales of the product to students or for home use.

Hardly another two weeks passed before he was back. "Look, we want to put a stop to this. So, just don't do any more work, OK?" Research was duly halted. Results obtained were made available to the company but it is a matter of speculation as to how useful they would be. Not only was this office products company in the grips of some serious procrastination but it also seemed to believe it already had all the answers, something its sales levels indicated it did not possess.

America Dreamin'

Another strange corollary to the Hurry Up and Wait style of decision making is avoiding information as an excuse for not taking action. This is a fairly common tactic among smaller organizations which dream big but fear big too. Many companies the world over aspire to sell to or enter the U.S. market but most will never take this step. They may even go so far as asking a supplier for a market research proposal, only to provide a string of excuses as to why they aren't going ahead with the work. A partner being sick, a shortage of funds, being too busy in the existing enterprise, all get trotted out.

What such companies are really doing is preserving their fantasy. If they were actually handed a concise analysis of the U.S. market, tailored to their particular product or circumstances, then they might have to act. They might have to follow through and actually attempt to enter the U.S. market. And then they might fail. Since this is all too real to contemplate, they remain in their comfort zone, dreaming, defining the information they need but never going any further, never making a decision.

Such were the tactics of a mid-level Canadian seminar or business conference company, which decided it wanted to enter the U.S. market for business seminars. Now, the company was smart enough to know the U.S. market is highly competitive so it decided more information was needed. In fact, the outside research supplier was told, in August of one year, that results were needed in a fairly tight timeframe, four weeks. Then, in September, the go-ahead was delayed only to be given in early December.

But, by mid-January, the seminar company was reneging on commitments to pay interim, agreed-upon billings and, sight unseen, had decided the information to be provided was of no value, not what it wanted.

What was really at work here, behind all the excuses and avoidance of bill paying, was a fear, fear of perhaps actually having to go forward and try and succeed in the U.S. Better to never take delivery of the data, since not having the information provides a ready-made excuse as to why a company never took the step. Rather than shoot the messenger, such companies practice blame the messenger.

Decision Drag

While procrastination is probably the biggest factor in decision avoidance, something known as "decision drag" is likely the next factor on the list. This is a phenomenon which occurs when too many people have to be in on a decision. Even when a company has gone out and obtained adequate information to support the decision, before it can actually be finalized and implemented, a great many constituents have to vet it. This can include employees (or "associates"), shareholders, suppliers, government bodies and customers. What can happen, when such decisions are dependent on information, is that by the time the decision is made, the underlying data is "bad" or out-of-date, simply because so much time has passed.

The ultimate form of such decision drag are the various public inquiries or judicial committee hearings which go on, supposedly to inform public policy development. Often, when such an exercise is completed, it leads to further inquiries, committees and hearings, so that any real decision is pushed away indefinitely. While input is important, when the input itself becomes the purpose and an excuse to delay, then the whole process has collapsed.

There is also a danger, with such processes, that the decision becomes watered-down so that an originally great idea turns into a mediocre one. Not the best route to profitability.

This is not to suggest that involving various constituents is a bad idea or that such consultations should be avoided — in the case of input from regulatory bodies, it may be mandatory — but it does suggest that companies need a process to allow for input while allowing the pace of decision making to proceed at a rate commensurate with the speed of the globalized economy. How this can occur is something we'll look at in Chapter 4 and return to again in Chapter 6 of this book.

Eye off the Future

This Hurry Up and Wait phenomenon is not restricted to decisions being made in the here and now; ignoring available information and delaying any kind of decision is also threatening the futures of many industries and professions.

Dentistry and dental surgeons are one example. There is a growing body of evidence, available today, that suggests mercury amalgam fillings may create severe health problems in some people, often crippling and debilitating conditions. Once such people have their fillings removed and replaced with non-mercury alternatives, their health is restored. Some dentists have seen "the writing on the wall" and have added the option of non-mercury fillings to their practices. But many other dentists have not. They even pooh-pooh the idea mercury amalgam fillings could have any link to toxicity in the body and consider the notion absurd.

How many of these dentists will still have a business in the 21st century remains to be seen, but they forget that what is ridiculed in one century becomes accepted practice in the next. Doctors ostracized the colleague who, in the 19th century, suggested doctors should wash their hands between patients as a way of stopping the spread of disease. How many doctors in the 20th century would even have a practice if they didn't follow this hygiene? It will be interesting to see how dentists making decisions about mercury fillings today fare in the decades ahead.

Heads in the Sand

This practice of "waiting and seeing" and taking no decision even though information indicating a decision urgently needs to be made is also true of companies making microwave ovens and microwave cooking accessories. The microwave oven has become such a fixture in so many homes that people forget it has not been around for that long and little is known about the longer term impact of preparing food this way.

What *is* known is that, for centuries, humans have cooked food, with external heat and by heating or cooking from the outside in. For millenia, this method suited the internal ecology of the human. Microwaving "cooks" by heating the water molecules in the food from the inside out. There are those who suggest this is not an ideal practice for humans and that the huge upswing in the use of the microwave has led to the re-emergence in the developed world of an old problem: parasites.

According to some sources, at least 85% of the North American population has parasites, worms and the like, to some degree but doesn't know it, although the debilitating health problems many people suffer can be traced to the health of their colon. And if the suspected link between this state of affairs and the emergence of microwave cooking is definitely established, the future will not look bright for microwave oven or cooking utensils manufacturers. Yet, if you ask them about this today, many will just shrug and say it's a bunch of nonsense. Just like the 19th century doctors on the subject of hand washing..

Who are the Main Culprits?

Whether the company taking the "Hurry Up and Wait" approach to decision making is large or small, most share one key attribute: they invariably are market followers not market leaders. Beyond the human foible of procrastination or the wishful thinking that, if they just wait long enough, the right information will miraculously appear, such companies are afraid to take decisions on their own. They would prefer if others in their industry "went first" and then they could follow suit. As such, they tend to also make decisions on a copycat basis.

What is the Cost of this Style of Decision Making?

Probably the most noticeable manifestation of Hurry Up and Wait decision making is slower growth. Since such companies delay making any decision — compared to others who take them for all the wrong reasons — they usually miss opportunities and, by the time they enter new markets, the opportunity to capitalize on the situation has passed, they can only imitate the leader or, the barriers to entry have become too high. Lower revenues and earnings are therefore the tangible cost.

In terms of intangible costs, the level of job creation by such companies tends to be lower, meaning there is a longer term cost to society.

Selected References

"A Smithsonian for Stinkers," *Business Week*, August 16, 1993, p. 82.
Barbarians at the Gate: The Fall of RJR Nabisco (1st Edition), Harper Collins/Harper Perennial, 1991.

"Canadian Tire Vows to Do it Right this Time" *Financial Post*, June 5, 1990, p. 3.

"Can This Chicken Fly?" *Restaurant Business*, May 1, 1996, p. 48–50.

"Downsizing Comes Back to Haunt a Brand," *Brandweek*, July 22, 1996, p. 40.

"Groupthink can be Fatal," *Information World*, April 14, 1997, p. 114.

"Has Pepsi Canned the Six-Pack?" *Marketing*, April 6, 1998, p. 12.

"He Who Mines Data may Strike Fool's Gold," *Business Week*, June 16, 1997, p. 40.

"Koo Koo Who?" *Forbes*, November 18, 1996, p. 80.

"Koo Koo Roo to Close DC Stores," *Nation's Restaurant News*, February 9, 1998, p. 4.

"Leasing Out Space Left by Corporate Downsizings," *New York Times*, November 9, 1997, p. 7.

"McDonald's: Can it Regain its Golden Touch?" *Business Week*, March 9, 1998, p. 70–77.

New Product Development: Managing and Forecasting for Strategic Success, John Wiley & Sons, 1993, p. 68–69.

"New Round of Layoffs May be Beginning," *Wall Street Journal*, November 13, 1997, p. A2.

"One Hundred Sixty Companies for the Price of One," *Forbes*, February 26, 1996, p. 56–59.

"Parasites," [ad] *Vitality Magazine*, April 1998, p. 8.

"Segmentation Nails the Smart Strategy," *Globe & Mail*, April 17, 1998, p. B23.

The Difference Between God and Larry Ellison, Hearst Book Group, October, 1997.

"The Importance of the list," *Teleprofessional*, February 1997, p. 14.

"The List: Big knives of 1997," *Business Week*, December 15, 1997.

"Drug Reactions Kill Thousands: Researchers," *Globe & Mail*, April 15, 1998, p. A3.

4 Information: The Key to Better Decisions

"A little learning is a dangerous thing
Drink deep or taste not the Pierian Spring
There shallow draughts intoxicate the brain
While drinking largely sobers us again."
Alexander Pope, 1711

The word "information" has become such a fixture in our modern lives that people rarely stop to think what it means. Its use in conjunction with "systems" and "technology" has led many to think that information is just about computers and networks.

This is unfortunate and also unfortunately far from the truth. Long before technology came along, "information" meant content: facts, figures, data, statistics, opinion, conjecture and many other forms. And, as described earlier, no state-of-the-art technology will save the day if content is weak or non-existent.

It is the need to become re-focussed on content, especially in decision making, that is one of the main reasons for writing this book. Information — regardless of its form or origin — is *the* key to better decisions, to reducing the waste and misery caused by poor business decision-making. If only a quarter of the bad business decisions being made today can be stopped by an input of the right information, any number of people will benefit.

Some people might laugh and say that this is a ridiculous proposition but they forget some of the recent history of error reduction. At one time, American industry accepted that several hundred television sets per 100,000 would be defective. Then the Japanese came along and aimed for a much lower error rate per 100,000, which eventually approached less than 0.1%. If errors in production can be reduced, so can errors in decision making.

What this chapter sets out to show is that information content can take many forms and needs a system or approach to its use. Good information work also requires a set of skills to retrieve, evaluate and analyze it. And what are these skills? What do information specialists — people trained in information as a separate discipline — know that others don't?

Rather than being attributable to a single ingredient, success in information work, on the content side, requires a whole recipe. There's formal training, as in graduate programs of library and information science, in journalism or other media, in communications and the presentation of information. There are qualities such as persistence and patience. There's knowhow gained in actually sourcing information and there's creativity, in how to go about finding information in the first place, especially if the target is proving an "elusive butterfly." These and other "tricks of the trade" are set out on the following pages.

Just What Do We Mean by Information? And Where and How do We Find it?

With all the emphasis on the "information age" and "knowledge workers", the word "information" has become overused. Any number of companies, from building materials suppliers to financial services companies have tagged the word "information" onto what they have to offer so that they, too, can say they are an "Information Company." (Information is trendy; the word implies by its very presence that a company is keeping pace with the times. And if the next big thing is turnips, then all such companies will undergo an immediate metamorphosis into being a Turnip Company!)

It's necessary to get off this information bandwagon and step back a bit to remember what information really is. There are many definitions and the issue can be hotly debated from many points of view, but in a business context, the simplest working definition is that information is "that which removes uncertainty." And by this information, is not necessarily meant just text or printed material on the page nor lines of data on a computer screen. Information can take many forms; sound recordings, film and video, radio broadcasts, in-person experiences (such as visiting tradeshow booths) and many other sources all provide information. A study was done showing that children use the crunchiness of potato chips, when they bite into them, as a source of information, to tell them whether the chips are fresh and therefore worth eating. All our organs of sense — taste, smell, touch, hearing and seeing — are information-gathering tools although it is this latter sense — sight — which we use the most in a literate culture, to obtain information.

Preparing for Information Work

Our earliest educational experience prepares us — or ideally, should prepare us — for this later role in adult life of working with information; from the time we enter school, we are exposed to the tools and practices of gathering and interpreting information and using it.

We learn to read, to write, to synthesize information from different sources and to present it to others. This is usually called a project or an essay. We may learn to present information in charts, pictures or by having to get up in front of our classmates to speak to them about it. If we are fortunate enough to attend good educational programs, the sources of information we learn to use include books and audio visual materials in the school library, films brought into the classroom, field trips, guests who come to speak at the school, etc. If we pursue our education in the field of higher learning, we may even learn how to design and conduct surveys, where we learn how to elicit feedback from individuals and obtain their opinion; our courses of study may also teach us other forms of field methods for information-gathering purposes, such as going overseas, as anthropologists do when they live with a tribe, to gather information in this way. Even conducting scientific experiments in the lab is an information gathering process, although many people might not see it this way.

Information in Business

The information available to businesses is similarly varied. It can be facts and figures, it can be opinion and forecasts, it can be statistics, estimates and rumors. It can include paid advertising and letters to the editor in trade publications, it can encompass promotional brochures and annual reports. In summary, it can include print material, electronic media (such as TV and films), computer-based databases and expert sources, which can include everyone at a company from the President on down to the receptionist, the delivery driver or the janitor. Given the wealth of information which is available, it is surprising and sad that so many business decision makers do not tap this resource and even sadder that often innocent people must suffer because of the poor decisions so taken.

Underlying Problems

As discussed earlier in this book, most people called upon to make decisions in business usually have expertise in disciplines other than information. Whether they are in operations, distribution, marketing, finance or another corporate function, most people in business have only the information training they acquired during either their compulsory education or during post-secondary education, all of which may have taken place 10, 15, or more years ago. Even those who have taken courses of study requiring research often confess to a fear of libraries or a dislike of the information gathering process. This can be equally true of professionals such as lawyers and accountants; more than one scientist has been known to confess that they chose scientific fields of endeavor because they didn't like writing essays. Five-hour labs at university were preferable to working on a ten-page paper any day.

Ironically, it is these very people who often find themselves in careers where they have to synthesize information — wherever it has come from — and present it to their peers or management, in spite of their aversion to the processes necessary in gathering and working with information. No wonder, then, that decisions often are made with a poor or non-existent foundation of information.

Not only do such individuals not know about the wealth of information sources actually available, they are often unfamiliar with the various approaches to rationalizing information and to systematize working with it. To them, it is all a massive sea in which they could easily drown.

Luckily for those untrained in information as a discipline, many who do work regularly with information gathering have not only gone down this path before but can help provide some structure as to how to go about this task, all of which is presented on the following pages.

Data vs. Information

One of the frequent debates, even among information specialists, is the difference between data and information and, beyond this, the distinction between intelligence, knowledge and wisdom.

Data is usually defined as a collection of facts, figures, statistics, etc. which have been organized but to which no analysis has been applied. Information is created when the data sets are combined or manipulated into patterns which represent logical connections. Intelligence is formed when insight is added to information; direction — the decisions to be made by the company — can then begin to be guided by this intelligence. Knowledge is the cumulative result of intelligence activity which brings a depth of understanding to a business problem. It gives management a sound basis for prudent decision making. Wisdom represents the zenith of the pyramid and the essence of a thoroughly analyzed knowledge base, providing an even more solid foundation for further action.

Secondary vs. Primary Sources

Some of this, of course, is a lofty aspiration and most readers of this book will need more practical frameworks to shape their gathering of data and use of information.

One of the models or approaches frequently used to bring some structure to the information gathering process is to classify sources of information as secondary or primary. This leads to terminology such as "secondary research," also known as "desk research" versus "primary research," which usually involves interviewing of human sources.

Secondary sources, as shown in Figure 4.1, include books, magazines, newsletters, recordings (such as film, TV or radio), databases — including material on the Web and Internet — annual reports, filings with regulatory bodies, and the like. Secondary sources are generally those where a certain amount or type of data has already been captured. Someone else has paid for the creation of these sources. They can generally be tapped via the library, a bookstore, for free (such as annual reports) or for a fee (such as government filings).

Secondary sources are those which have given rise to the expression "information overload"; they are plentiful but, having been prepared or assembled for a wide audience, rarely can answer in full specific questions to support business decision making. (People who think otherwise are usually those who practice question migration as discussed earlier in Chapter 2).

Most researchers who work professionally in business only use such secondary sources as a starting point. They recognize — usually based on experience — that there are limitations in such sources when precise answers are sought. That's why they generally embark on primary research, whether by way of surveys, using structured questionnaires or by one-on-one interviews

SECONDARY	PRIMARY
Books	Academics
Magazines	Association staff
Journals	Journalists
Newsletters	Business owners
Conference proceedings	Union representatives
Theses	Store managers
Films	Customer service reps
Videos	Technicians
Radio broadcasts	Sales people
TV programs	Company presidents
Online databases	Board directors
Annual reports	Computer specialists
Product literature	Retail clerks
Promotional material	Receptionists
Handbooks	Executives
Manuals	Engineers
Encyclopedias	Scientists
Textbooks	Professionals
Government filings	Product designers
Blue prints ... and more	Janitors ... and more

Figure 4.1   Secondary Versus Primary Sources

with what are termed expert sources (which can include anyone ranging from a Ph.D. at a university down to the customer service rep at a company); "expert" here is relative to the information sought. If someone is researching materials-handling equipment, truck drivers may have far more expertise to share than university professors.

Open Sources

Since no single approach to rationalizing information is better than any other, it is important for readers interested in gaining a better understanding of this topic to understand as many models as possible.

A frequently used term, particularly by the intelligence operatives of the military, is "open sources", meaning much of the wealth of published or public domain data described in the discussion of secondary sources. However, in this model, open sources can also include human or expert sources (sometimes referred to as "humint" for human intelligence) who are at liberty to divulge information.

Hard vs. Soft Information

It is precisely because a source is only as good as its original purpose that other approaches or models for information gathering have evolved. One of these is to create a spectrum of sources ranging from hard to soft.

In this approach, "hard" sources, as shown in the Figure 4.2, are those which capture and record factual and statistical data, usually of a retrospective nature. Moving along the spectrum, the sources become less retrospective and "softer," until the spectrum moves into sources which are entirely "soft": opinion, rumor, gossip, conjecture, etc. These sources tend to be indicative and point up trends and future direction.

Another way to look at this spectrum is to see a continuum from more quantitative sources to the qualitative. Both have a role to play in information work but each needs to be relied upon according to its inherent strengths; hard sources are great for quantifying the way things have been in the past while soft sources are ideal for indicating the trends emerging which will

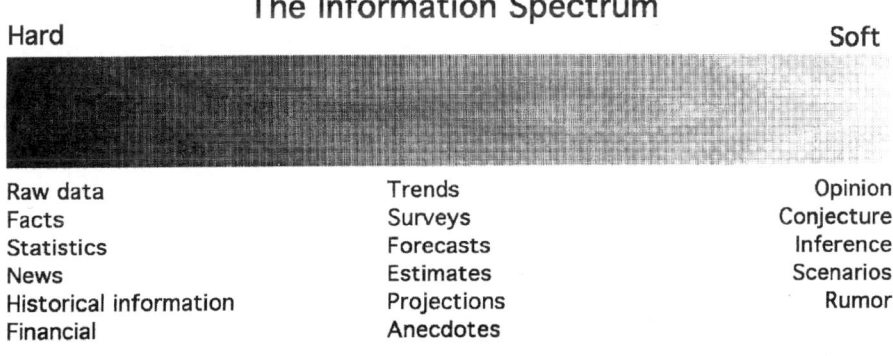

The Information Spectrum

Hard		Soft
Raw data	Trends	Opinion
Facts	Surveys	Conjecture
Statistics	Forecasts	Inference
News	Estimates	Scenarios
Historical information	Projections	Rumor
Financial	Anecdotes	

Figure 4.2   The Information Spectrum

shape the future. Just as these soft sources cannot be used to describe the past, hard sources cannot be used as a reliable predictor of the future.

Pyramid Structures

Beyond categorizing sources as secondary or primary, hard or soft, open or closed, it is possible to both categorize them *and* organize them into a structure suited for information retrieval, by creating a pyramid, which is broader at the base and narrower at the top, mainly in the form of an isosceles triangle. In this triangle, with its steep narrow sides (Figure 4.3), public domain information represents the base of the pyramid while less available or more private sources of information are placed at the top. As an information seeker moves during the research process from the base of the pyramid to the top he or she encounters fewer sources of information which are easy to access and finds that it is necessary to tap more creative approaches to gathering information to obtain the answers sought.

Spiralling in on Your Target

Yet another approach to organizing or rationalizing information is to see it on a spiral, where sources more peripheral to the target questions are placed on the circumference around the outside of the spiral and sources which are more relevant or closely tied to the target are placed on the inner whorls of the spiral as you move toward the center.

Figure 4.4 shows the sources which might be tapped and the sequence in which they might be tapped if the exercise was to build a profile of a company. In this example, the sources are all primary sources but it would be equally possible to create a spiral with just secondary sources or a mix of primary and secondary.

Tactical vs. Strategic

Information in sources can also be systematized or organized for information gathering along a spectrum of how easy or difficult they are to obtain and their relevance to tactical versus strategic business decisions. As is shown in Figure 4.5, readily available information — the secondary or open sources referenced above — tends to be of greatest value in tactical decision making; to find information of value to issues surrounding business strategy —

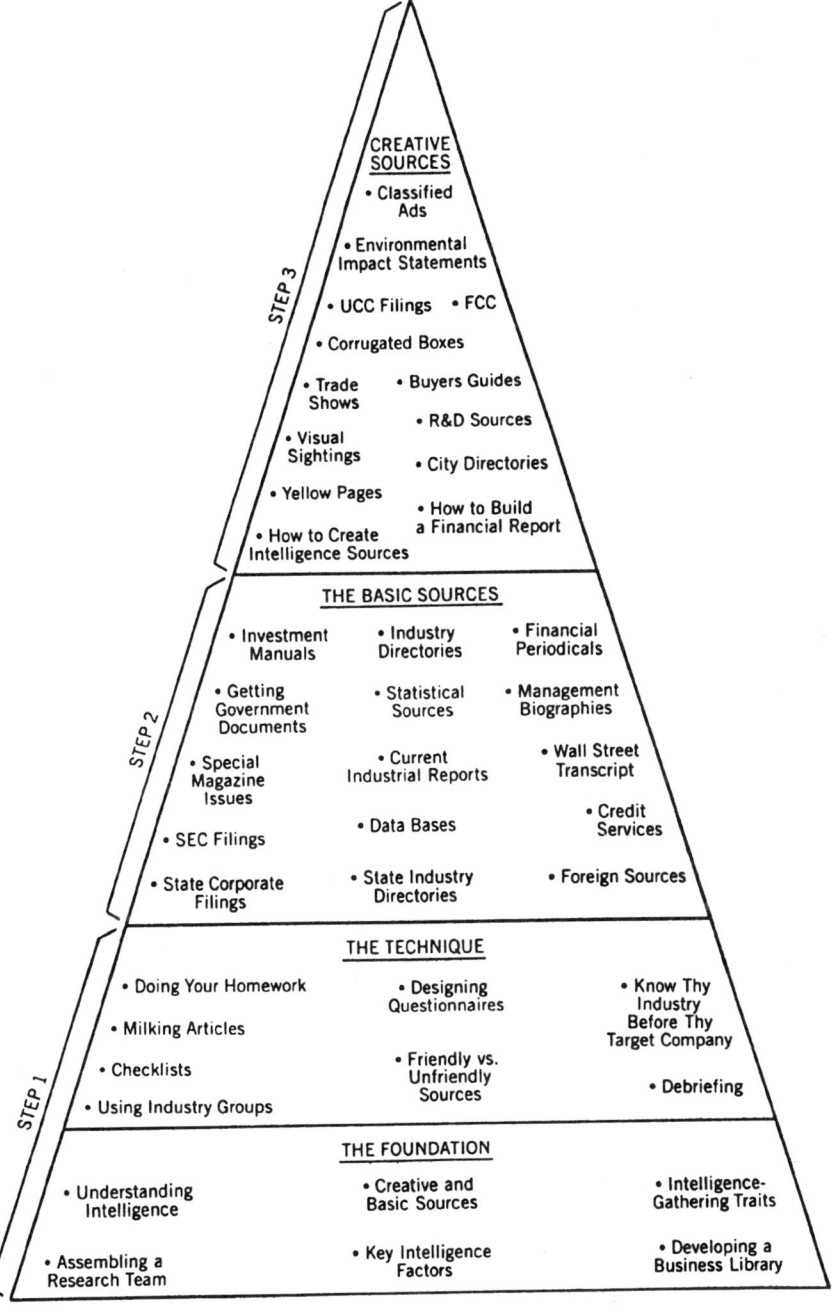

Figure 4.3   The Intelligence Gathering Pyramid

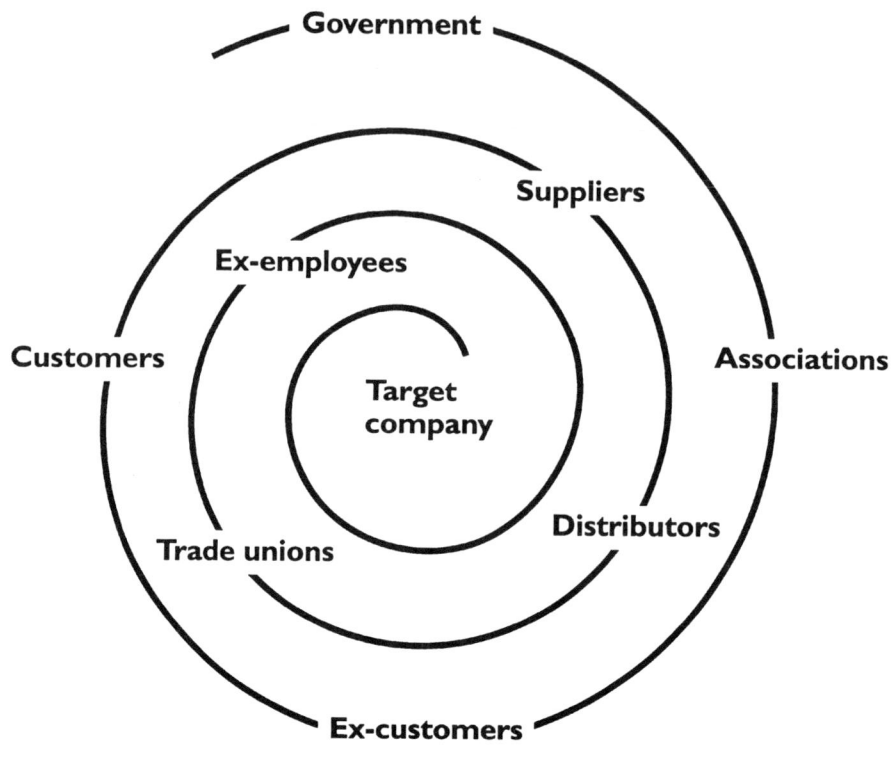

Figure 4.4   The Information Spiral

whether to formulate your own strategy or understand another organization's strategy — it is usually necessary to turn to interviews.

What these and other models of information help achieve is provide some sort of structure or rationalization for approaching information, given how much is being created. In some cases, the type of question and the type of answer sought will determine whether you look for statistical data that has historical perspective or turn to talking to expert sources to get a sense of unmet needs, for example, in terms of the products they need. Instead of allowing someone to drown in the vast sea of information which exists, these models provide a compass for getting to the shore.

External vs. Internal Information

Most of the models presented focus on information that is externally created or gathered (e.g., by publishers or government) or externally available

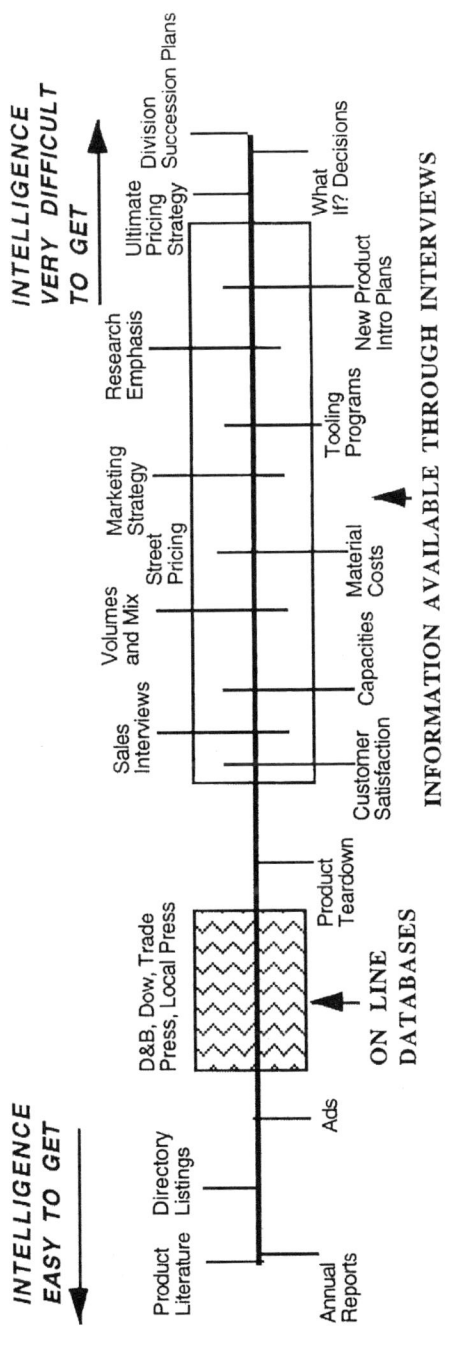

Figure 4.5   The Electromagnetic Business Intelligence Spectrum

(e.g., from expert human sources). Where does this leave the vast amount of internal information collected and assembled by companies? Many corporations, especially large, Top 500 concerns, are huge repositories of information of all sorts.

Internal information should not be overlooked but only if its use does not lead the company to commit the first deadly sin of decision making, namely, believing: "We Already Have All The Answers."

It is often true that, in addition to formal collections of internal information — corporate libraries, databases, information systems, etc. — companies have a wealth of informal or unsystematized information, in the form of their employees' collective and individual knowledge. In fact, trying to get at this knowledge and leverage it has led to a focus on "knowledge management" and creation of "Chief Knowledge Officer" positions at companies. While some see this as a fad, it does point up the lack of emphasis companies have often placed, in the past, on employees' experiences and insights, especially more junior or lower ranked personnel. Starting to pay attention to this issue is unquestionably positive.

However, companies need equally to guard against too much reliance — even in the excitement of doing something as innovative and trendy as knowledge management — on internal sources; the danger here is in becoming a closed-loop, believing you have all the answers and Hearing No Evil from the outside world. For practical purposes, both internal and external information sources should be valued and sought out.

How Do You Get Started? How Do You Know When You Have Enough Information?

The two main information-related problems which face the business decision maker are knowing, first, how to get started on the search and then knowing when he or she has enough information. And because most executives and managers are specialized in a discipline other than information, this is not an easy task.

There is also enough confusion surrounding sources of information that it is easy to understand why the person untrained in information work can fall victim to not having the right information, even though they set out to retrieve it. Then, the untrained person may know only the most rudimentary information retrieval skills or may not have kept up-to-date on newer sources.

Whatever tactics served people adequately in the past, many are not suitable for survival in an information age; even believing you can rely on a source such as the Internet — choc-a-bloc as it is with misinformation and disinformation — will jeopardize a company's success in a Knowledge Economy.

Are You Ready to Gather Information?

Before anyone does set out to gather information to support decision making, it's a good idea to make sure the decisions which have to be made have at least been formulated. While flexibility — allowing new questions onto the agenda and modifying existing questions in the light of discoveries — is extremely important, there at least has to be an initial set of objectives formulated.

Sometimes this may take the form of problem definition. "Our sales are down 25% in the Southwest. Why?" or "Where can we find new markets for our existing premium widgets?" Once the problem has been fully dissected — and it may take an infusion of information to reach this stage — the decisions to be made will emerge, likely necessitating even more research. At other times, the decision that has to be made will already have been formulated. "Since our lease won't be renewed, we have to find new premises" or "Our 20 year old equipment has to be replaced".

Often, the statement of a problem or decision which has to be made gives birth to a whole series of questions which have to be answered. "If our sales are down, what has happened to our known competitors' sales in the same market?" "Have new competitors entered the market?" "What changes have occurred to the customer base in that market?" "How is the economy doing down there?" Only by answering these questions will the framework for further decision making emerge.

But without this initial "pre-decision" step, successful information gathering cannot proceed.

What About the Type of Research?

Once the decisions have been identified, before any actual information can be sourced, some consideration needs to be given to the type of research methodology to be used. An in-depth review of all research methodologies is beyond the scope of this book but an overview is not for, here again, is another of the traps into which the untrained tend to fall.

Earlier, we referred to secondary versus primary sources of information; this dichotomy also defines the two principal arms or avenues of research, secondary research versus primary research. Not unsurprisingly, what's known as secondary research relies exclusively on secondary sources, hence the reason for its other name: desk research, although the "desk" may be in someone's office, at a library or under a computer terminal.

Primary research, which can also go under the moniker "original research" usually involves "leg work" or the undertaking of interviews and research in the field or over the phone: interviewing people, visiting sites, getting a hands-on feel for a process.

Most people believe — mainly because they have never seen any evidence to the contrary — that all research is market research of the type conducted by surveys with what are known as closed-ended questions and that this, plus the type of information produced, is the only option. These are the type of surveys most consumers are familiar with, where someone calls at home and asks: How often does your household purchase tomato soup? How many cans do you use per meal? Which is your preferred brand? Anyone who takes the time to respond to such surveys can almost hear the survey interviewer checking off the little boxes on the form (which nowadays is on a computer screen). Most consumers who do participate in such surveys have probably felt frustration when an answer they provide doesn't "fit" a box and has to be migrated to the next best available.

An extension of this is the type of survey where respondents are asked to rank their experiences, either by numbers 1 to 5 or 1 to 10, or by pre-selected answers: Excellent, Good, Fair, or Poor. Again, if the respondent's answer doesn't conform to the pre-selections, there is often no scope, with this approach, to record whatever the respondent does have to share.

These survey or research methods are commonly used because it is easy to process the answers when they are captured in this form. It is also easier to create pie charts and bar graphs with percentages which neatly add up to 100% this way. While there is nothing wrong with taking a numeric or quantitative approach to research, it is not the only way.

Before setting out on any information gathering or research exercise, decision makers therefore also need to look at the decisions to be made and whether or not certain methodologies will produce the right answers. Want to know about quantities purchased or planned volumes to be ordered? Numeric methods of information gathering are ideal. Want to know why key customers stopped buying or why a competitor has exited a market when you haven't? Numeric methods won't do at all. The more behind-the-scenes the information sought, the more you want to get at the why, the process, the rationale of events, the more in-depth, open-ended questions need to be used for interviewing, the greater the need to combine secondary or public domain sources with primary or interview sources.

Will the Information be Filtered?

Equally important, in evaluation of various research methods open to you, is determining how close they will keep you to the results. Surveys, as described above, are often structured to produce outcomes which are easy to analyze and present. Beware, in such cases, of too much "pie-chartism," results which are gussied up in graphics rather than being presented as raw data. Sometimes you want access to both; the more information is run through a series of filters before it reaches you, the more likely you'll end up committing one of the Seven Deadly Sins, notably Hear No Evil or All Aboard the Bandwagon. Except, in such cases, it won't be because you didn't set out to gather information; it will have more to do with how it's presented to you.

Single Sourced Information

Once either the decisions to be made have been defined or the questions to be answered have been formulated, some form of secondary research is likely to be the first step. But, here, the process is likely to bog down if the people doing the information gathering — either the decision makers or people delegated by them for the task — don't tap the right sources or enough sources. In Chapter 4, we looked at various models for rationalizing the vast number of sources available or sequences for tapping them; an additional layer to this is the extent to which questions can be answered by a single source or need a multiple source solution.

One of the key failings is to believe, as many business people do, that all the answers are in a database. According to this theory, all you have to do, to get the information you need, is to hit a few buttons on the keyboard and out it all pops. Nowadays, some people even firmly believe that the Internet has all the information they will ever need. As will be discussed, these sources are as rife with errors as print sources ever were, perhaps more so.

Others, harking back to an earlier era, rely on their trade association and never look further than the information emanating from such a source.

The Dangers of One-Stop Shopping

Some questions can be safely answered by such a single source approach; for example, if you want to know the temperature in Madrid, Spain prior to a trip, there are several sources you can tap, such as an encyclopedia, a travel agent, a consular office or embassy, etc. But you only need tap one; the reason for this is the nature of the information sought. The same is true if you want the figure for the number of housing starts in the U.S. last year; several government, association and corporate sources have that answer, leaving you free to tap any one of them.

But very few important business decisions can be made with this "one-stop shopping" approach; to make most business decisions correctly, multiple sources of information will need to be tapped, usually via secondary *and* primary research, given that the question asked is very rarely a simple question but is rather more likely a series of inter-connected questions. If we build the new factory, how much capacity will we be able to utilize? Are the markets for the products it will make growing or declining? What are our competitors' plans: are they adding capacity as well? If so, what will that do to prices? Such questions represent only the tip of the iceberg of those which have to be asked; it should not surprise anyone therefore to learn that answering them will take much more than a quick search on the Internet or a trip to a single library. In fact, a lot of the key information to answer such questions is not recorded, meaning it is not in print, not in a database, not on the Internet. Such information often exists in the heads of the expert sources referenced earlier.

One-Step, Two-Step, Multi-Step

Another way to get started on secondary research is to analyze the questions you have to ask in terms of how many steps it will take to answer them. Reference librarians have long had a way of categorizing reference questions into what are termed one-step, two-step and multi-step questions. The one-step questions which come to the reference desk are those for which the librarian already knows the location of the answer; these are the kinds of questions which can be answered by turning to a dictionary, an encyclopedia (whether print or CD–ROM), an almanac or a similar publication. The two-step questions are those which involve going to either the card catalog or its on-line cousin, to look up the source of the information, hence the two steps. The multi-step reference questions, as the name suggests, require several steps to answer them, usually involving tapping a range of sources in the library and possibly elsewhere. As suggested earlier, most of the more important decisions in business are really multi-step questions which need to tap multiple sources for the answer, again drawing on both secondary and primary research.

Sequencing Sources

Equally important, in determining the number of sources to be tapped and the steps necessary to tap them, is to recognize this is not just a quantitative exercise, that tapping 10 sources is not better than 5, nor 20 better than 10. As information specialists can explain, one of the secrets of successful information work is how you weave the sources together; it may be more fruitful, at times, to tap expert sources only once secondary sources have been exhausted. At other times, a search will only be successful if you tap the expert sources first and then use their knowledge as a guide to secondary source material.

Although the models shown earlier in this chapter presented options for approaching and using information, the objectives of the search determine not only *which* sources but in *what sequence*. To use Figure 4.4 as an example, if creating a profile of a particular company is the objective, if understanding more about that company is key to a successful decision, then the company itself moves to the center of the spiral. But if a trade union, for example, was the object of study, then the union would move to the core of the spiral and the company — or several which deal with the union — would move to the outer whorls of the spiral.

How Long Should It take?

Given the tendencies of business to first timetable deadlines for decisions and *then* seek information to support them — a practice which will not serve companies well in the information-dependent 21st century — this is a very key question. It is also something of a "How Long is a Piece of String?" question.

The answer, of course, depends on what is being sought. A search for information could take anywhere from 2 weeks to 2 years. So, while there isn't a handy answer, there is a good rule of thumb: a search will always take twice as long as you think it will.

Another yardstick to use is to look — honestly — at the likelihood someone else has asked such questions in the past, leading to the pre-assembling of the answers. Encyclopedias, whether print or CD–ROM, have their existence predicated on a history of certain questions being asked and continuing to be asked. Every year there is a child somewhere doing a project on sharks or elephants, so there is adequate coverage of these topics. Every year, someone decides to visit the City of Light for the first time, so Paris is discussed in detail. The information they contain thus addresses a commonality of questions.

But if you are introducing a new product, for which there is no history, chances are there will be no shortcut to the answers. Little or nothing will have been compiled and piecing together the information which is available will take time. To be on the safe side, in business, think months rather than days to answer most of the questions which come up.

The Likelihood of Outcomes

Another step to take, in addition to estimating timeframes for the information search, is to assess if there will likely be a lot of information available or only a little on the topic you have at hand as is likely the case, as just mentioned, if your topic is very new. Here, there is a quick rule of thumb which can be used and that is: how willing or able are people to pay to have this information created?

One of the reasons it is often difficult to make informed decisions about expansions overseas is that in some countries, there are not enough funds to allocate to activities such as central statistical gathering of the kind handled by the Census Bureau and similar central agencies found in countries in the developed world. If a nation or society cannot afford information gathering and the whole infrastructure of information work, there will likely be less information available on the topic in readily available sources. This doesn't mean that the information cannot be obtained, it just means that it will be a time-consuming process and will require exclusively primary research, often on-site in the target country. In the case of wealthy, industrialized nations, where there are significant publishing industries, producers of alternate media sources, such as CD–ROMs, and a whole infrastructure of government offices, libraries, associations and other groups in the business of gathering and disseminating information, then the likelihood of the outcome is much better than for any such excursion in a developing country.

Reaching Information Sufficiency

This suggests the length of time any information search will take is a function of both the questions which have to be answered and the resources available to answer them.

It also suggests that the point at which "Information Sufficiency" is reached will vary from search to search and decision to decision. And there are no firm yardsticks to measure when this point of sufficiency is reached although there are some guidelines which come into play.

Information sufficiency has usually been achieved when the information being turned up becomes repetitive or the same answers are heard over and over. It only takes a couple of sources, for example, to show that the temperature in Madrid falls into predictable ranges at given times of the year. Information sufficiency can be achieved fairly quickly for such searches. The same is true of housing starts; one or two unrelated sources providing overlapping answers mean that there is no point in going further. New information found will not deviate much from the figures already retrieved.

Of course, with more complex questions — or series of questions — the answers will not be found as quickly. But here, again, there are indicators. If there are only ten companies in an industry and each has a fairly similar market and market share, speaking to four or five might be indicative of market and customer trends, obviating the need to interview them all.

Knowing When to Stop

Getting started on the information search — and persuading business decision makers that this should be an automatic part of any decision made — is only part of the equation. It is equally important to know when to stop gathering information. For example, are there searches which will just never produce a substantial amount of information?

This can be true for example, if you have invented a new product for which there is no existing parallel and no substitutable market; sometimes you will not find a lot of published or secondary information and may not even be able to gather much from primary research interviews.

As indicated, one of the tip-offs that you are ready to stop the research process is when you start to encounter a fair level of repetition. If you have conducted 20 interviews with knowledgeable industry sources about market conditions and they are all saying pretty much the same thing, with no opportunity for collusion, this suggests that you are getting to the answer and no new research discoveries will be made. When multiple sources give the same facts over and over, so the answer is only reinforced by subsequent research, it suggests there is no need to go on and these targets can be eliminated from the search. This allows you to streamline and focus on the balance of the targets.

System vs. Serendipity

One last note of caution to anyone before they embark on an information search: The greatest system for seeking out information will only get you so far. Sometimes, key pieces of information will come up more by serendipity. You may be diligently researching customer opinion about a newly introduced product and why it is not selling well, but it is a chance remark by the waitress at the diner or the parking lot attendant which provides the clue you need. Or, it may be something in print in a publication quite unconnected with the topic you are searching: a problem with a chemical compound may swim into a new focus based on something you read about nail polish remover in a beautician's trade magazine. The important thing is to remember this can happen and be alert to it.

What to Do when You Don't Have Enough?

Earlier chapters of this book discussed some of the sins which business decision makers commit, such as: thinking you have all the answers; asking the wrong questions; and otherwise short changing the role of information in decision making.

Usually, these mistakes stem from not bothering to gather any information but the decision making process can also be derailed when someone starts off, with the best of intentions, to gather information but cannot find enough. Here again, the fact many business decision makers are not trained in information work has an effect. Having tapped all the predictable sources of information they can think of, such people find themselves high and dry. It is easy in such circumstances to decide there is no information whereas this is rarely the case. What becomes a key skill here — and an important part of the decision making process — is the ability to assess what is missing and determine where it might be. This requires a realistic appraisal as to whether the information is "gettable" and at what cost.

Pre-empt the Problem

Perhaps the first tactic to ensure adequate information does result from searches to support decision-making is to pre-empt as many problems as possible before they arise.

Sending inexperienced researchers to handle the task is one surefire way to create troubles and end up with insufficient information, as people not used to the "cut and thrust" of the research process may miss sources or give up too soon. This state of affairs occurs more often than might be expected and at some surprisingly large corporations. Again, the "glamor" of research, the fact many people find the idea of information gathering "fascinating" weighs in, with such eager volunteers being assigned to the task.

Lest this sound like a pitch for using outside research firms, companies need to consider the evolutionary dimensions of information work, especially as concerns content. Earlier in this book, comparisons were made to advertising and public relations and how, once upon a time, these were either viewed as "soft" costs or expenditures which could be avoided. Over time, of course, the professionalism of both advertising and public relations grew, so that their distinct methodologies became more recognized and the practice of taking on outside counsel in these disciplines more accepted. Many companies are still on their way up the learning curve in how they perceive the discipline of information gathering and the practice of taking on either in-house or outside expertise.

One-Shot or Ongoing?

Another way companies are still on their way up the information learning curve — and this can equally restrict the amount of information they enjoy — is by fixating on project based or one-shot research, rather than seeing this activity as an ongoing one.

Although the world — competitors, markets, customer needs, supplier availability and more — changes daily, companies still think that a three week analysis of a competitor or a new market will somehow "do them" for the next five years! (And, heck, if you'd just spent $10,000, you'd expect the report to last that long too!)

This view of the world just isn't realistic. A report about a competitor only provides a snapshot, a moment frozen in time. A study of a market is, by definition, more retrospective than forward-looking, however many predictions it contains. Most data is out of date — or proven partly inaccurate — very quickly. This is why companies, for the 21st century, have to make a sizeable mind-shift to ongoing investment in all manner of information, even if they might not use it all.

And sticking resolutely to a project-based approach is only one of the ways to short circuit the availability of enough information for decision-making.

Search Sabotage

Other ways to sabotage the process is to insist on too narrow a search or to set up inadequate budgets for the task, which are often interrelated.

Many business decision makers think they will be clever, especially if they belong to the "saving money" school of decision making. Insisting that only secondary source searches be conducted is one way; this is rather like believing in the old adage of making a silk purse out of a sow's ear. As discussed in Chapter 4, such secondary sources are often designed to meet a range of more general purposes and are not targeted to solve the particular problems of your corporation. This is why they are best used as a starting point. Refusing to allow primary research to be undertaken or setting up too small a budget for any interviewing will doom most business information searches to failure, creating a situation where the information obtained is not enough to make the decision at hand.

This was what happened to a company interested in expanding into the U.K. They wanted to target medical rehabilitation equipment distributors but didn't want to pay more than $100 for the list. While names and addresses which supposedly met their requirements could be obtained for this figure, the lack of a budget to doublecheck and verify appropriateness confounded later sales efforts. That's because such "ready-made" lists rely on codings, whether SIC codes or some other system, which the companies on the list themselves select. What most people fail to realize is that companies often assign inaccurate codes to themselves. Or worse, codes that were once accurate continue to be used, even though the business has changed its line of work. Whereas at one time, someone senior filled out the form for the directory or list compiler, this task is now delegated to a more junior staff person who is merely instructed to note any changes, such as address, and send the form back.

Who Else Needs to Know?

Even when precautions have been taken before information gathering begins, problems can arise. In most business information gathering exercises, when researchers come up dry after tapping the more predictable sources, they can usually get the research process back on track by asking: who else needs to know? For an example, who else needs to know housing start projections? Who else needs to know what the temperature is in Madrid? Who else needs to know if our competitors are increasing capacity? Who else needs to know...? The answer to the "who else?" question will vary from situation to situation and takes imagination, more than a knowledge of sources, to answer it. As there are entire books devoted to the subject of sources of information, this book will not dwell on an enumeration of sources but rather will provide some rules of thumb.

To answer the "who else?" question in just about all situations, you need to look at the underlying motives other people or groups might have for going out, seeking and then compiling the information. To use the housing starts example mentioned above, governments have a great need to know and track housing starts because it indicates the potential for future tax generation, especially at the municipal level. Economists like to know about housing starts because this is one of the bellwethers of the economy. Associations representing suppliers of building materials like to know about housing starts, because it indicates a future opportunity for their members.

Although secondary sources have their limitations in response to very specific questions corporations have, their very abundance does create many possibilities of "who else" might know or "where else" the information might be. Information overload is not entirely a bad thing; it is just a matter of finding ways to cut through it.

Even if the national business press has nothing to offer about a company, product or market under investigation, dozens of other sources might. There are local newspapers which circulate only around the town where they are published (which may just be where your target company is located), there are special focus newsletters, regional trade magazines and more. Unless a topic is so new, so unheard of, that no one has discussed it, there is always a "who else" or "where else" to turn to.

Even questions which might seem to skirt into highly confidential areas can often be answered with creativity and imagination. A competitor may wish to expand its facility and do so quietly, so your organization won't know that the competitor's capacity is about to double and put you at a disadvantage in the marketplace. But there are very few jurisdictions these days where someone can construct a building or an extension without leaving a paper trail. Look again closely at the motives; while the competitor's motive is to keep things as hush-hush as possible, the local municipality is interested in having the construction properly documented, citizens in neighboring areas want to know about the impact of the new building, environmental "watch dogs" may want to know what the impact of the facility will be, etc. And these motives are all equally as strong as your competitor's to keep things quiet.

This illustrates that, even with primary sources, there is always a "who else" or "where else" to turn to. The local municipality likely has employees administering documentation, such as building permits and blueprints; they can prove a valuable source of information. Citizens groups who take a keen interest in what happens in their neighborhood may have actually walked or driven past the site and have anecdotes to share. Environmental watch-dog organizations may track large corporations or other entities which regularly construct new facilities; they may have someone on staff who can relate a range of experiences with the target organization.

Have You "Milked" Your Source Today?

If, in spite of taking these steps, the information available still seems inadequate, it may be time to see what else you can do with what you already have. Professional researchers sometimes refer to this as "milking" sources.

By going through any information which has been obtained, further leads can usually be found. Are there sources or references, such as a bibliography, at the end of the article or journal paper? Who is quoted in the article? Which organizations are referenced? Secondary sources nearly always lead to more.

The same procedure can be used with primary sources. Even if a contact seems like a long-shot, it's always worth a call because they may know someone else to whom you can be referred. All interactions with primary sources should end with a question such as: Who else do you recommend we speak with?

The Importance of Timing

Results which are still less than satisfactory may also owe their condition to the timing of when the research was undertaken. Depending on the industry, there are times of the year which are better than others to gather information. Targeting the managed turf business (golf courses and the like)? Want to interview farmers? Forget January; this is often the only time of year such people can take holidays. Interested in tenniswear or the tennis industry? Forget the two weeks when Wimbledon is running; many people take time off then.

The same is true of the timing of any industry's major conference event; entire companies seem to empty out while those left to "man the fort" are too busy for research surveys or to send out information.

Companies or organizations which have just gone through or are in the process of downsizing or re-organizing also present poor targets in terms of timing. In such situations, people may be unclear as to their duties or there may be no one assigned to a particular function.

Timing can also be a factor if not enough time has been allowed for the search, a not uncommon scenario, particularly when decision makers like to fly-by-the-seat-of-their pants.

A global chemical company headquartered in the mid-west set out to gather information on 12 equally global competitors as to the business direction for these companies over the next 5 years. While there was an abundance of public domain information — almost too much in fact — since all the targets were large publicly traded entities, there was barely enough time for the task: three weeks. It took almost that long to gather the print and database material never mind read it. Then, senior executives had to be interviewed at each company; to track down and interview just one can take three weeks.

It was more by luck than judgment that the chemical company obtained the quality of information it did. But given the importance of the exercise — company staffers were using the information to recommend strategic direction and select business initiatives for the next 5 to 10 years — it was a precarious way to go about the task.

That's why, if results produce poor information or no information, it may be just as well to consider how timing might be a factor and to wait a while and conduct the research over, when timing is more favorable.

The Passage of Time

If timing of information gathering can affect the quality of results, the passage of time can have a bearing on what's available as well. Although business tends to be forward-looking, sometimes the answers to questions are rooted in the past, too much so.

The experience of a California-based petroleum processor interested in learning about competitors' operations based in the eastern U.S. illustrates this. Requests for documents such as blueprints, placed with government under Freedom of Information (FOI) legislation, turned up dry. Yet the competitors all had huge operations, campuses which sprawled for miles, with activities having multiple sorts of environmental impacts. However, these facilities had been operating for many years and pre-dated FOI by decades. At the time they were built, there had been no requirements to file. And, in the case of where there had been requirements, such as building permits, records had not been kept this far back.

In such a case, there was little the refiner could do to offset the lack of materials.

Were the Objectives Realistic?

If, after taking corrective action, a search is still coming up dry, then it may be time to re-assess the objectives and how realistic they were. This can often be a stumbling block if the objectives and the questions raised were ahead of their time. A marketing vice president at a manufacturing company had the idea that his company should turn the marketing department into a stand-alone profit center, with him at the helm.

A search for examples of companies which had already taken this step, ideally in manufacturing environments, was undertaken. The problem was, very few companies had undertaken anything similar and some of those which had, had abandoned the scheme as unworkable. In such a case, very little information was produced, meaning the vice president had to turn to other strategies to make his case for a profit center decision. (To give him his due, he didn't "shoot the messenger!")

Do You Have a Process?

Ending up with insufficient information to make a decision may also indicate a company doesn't have a process for utilizing information fully in decision making. The first characteristics of such a process should be to be proactive and position the company to anticipate information that will be needed and to otherwise keep ahead of trends and developments which can have an impact on the business, whether positive or negative. Such a forward-looking orientation will usually address at least 50% of the gaps which otherwise occur when information gathering to support decision making is undertaken in reactive mode.

The next part of the process is to identify the magnitude of the decision and have a pre-determined level of effort decided. For example, decisions requiring expenditures can be tiered by the dollars to be spent or by the impact on the organization, such as one location only or enterprise-wide. The greater the magnitude of the expenditure or the greater the impact on the overall organization, the more information needs to be gathered. Obviously, less information is needed to purchase paper clips than a fleet of new vehicles; likewise, a decision about the cafeteria at one location won't have the same impact as a new benefits plan affecting thousands of employees.

Likewise, the magnitude of the decision has a bearing on how many constituents need to be involved in the process, before the decision has to be taken. Sometimes, canvassing such constituents before the information gathering even starts can ensure buy-in and commitment so that subsequent research and decision making can proceed relatively quickly and unfettered.

Taking these steps, will either eliminate or seriously reduce the number of situations where the information available is inadequate to the decision making task at hand.

How To Evaluate What You Have

As already discussed, one of the reasons people have perhaps not always been diligent in obtaining information to support decision making is the sheer quantity of the stuff that is available, the widely documented "information overload." And even when information has been gathered to support a decision, because of this issue of volume, there is always an attendant issue of quality to be resolved; is what you've gathered good enough for the purposes you have?

Again, when non-specialists are the ones evaluating the information, there is an even greater danger that insufficient scrutiny will be applied. It is far easier to rationalize that the information to decide about a market expansion is OK or "will do" than to give it a hard look, see all its inadequacies and then go out and do more research. Even companies which take the time and trouble to conduct research or commission it from an independent party can fall prey to this all too human weakness — not wanting to do something over or to do something further. We are all lazy souls at heart!

But given the high costs of making the wrong decision, finding ways to evaluate the information as to its reliability is key. Can it be trusted? What doesn't add up? These and other questions must be asked — and answered.

The Answer is Only as Reliable as the Source

One of the more important questions about reliability is: Where did the information come from? There's an old saying about something coming "straight from the horse's mouth" and this is a very important yardstick to use in evaluating business data. Who was the source? How close to the source was the information found? What motives might the source have had for distorting or embellishing the truth? A quick look back at the spiral model of information discussed in the section on "Just What Do We Mean by Information?" shows how sources of information are closer or further away from the particular target. Such distance or proximity can distort the information and affect its quality. Likewise, information that is filtered through a channel, such as a reporter at a newspaper, has a greater chance of being inaccurate, simply because the words used to convey the information originally have now been filtered through someone else's understanding of the situation and then re-worded, using the reporter's vocabulary, in the process of publication. This does not mean the information will be totally inaccurate; it just means that some distortion may have entered the picture.

Fact Checking

Other measures of the degree of reliability and accuracy can be found in the level of editing and fact-checking to which a source has been subjected. Major trade and business publications, for example, often have what's known as a copy editing department, where each and every fact is doublechecked both with the original source and with independent sources. Smaller publications often lack the financial resources for this and so must rely on the reporter's or writer's level of accuracy. This means that hearsay may remain in an article when it should have been edited out; it can also mean that transpositions of figures, which turn $101 million into $110 million are not caught. Such errors can lead decision makers to make the wrong decisions, with the magnitude of the error in direct proportion to the magnitude of the typographical error.

These are just some of the pitfalls of the Internet and the World Wide Web, which so many people believe to be above suspicion. There is little fact checking or copy-editing.

Multiple Viewpoints

Another indicator of the degree of reliability is whether or not multiple sources or points-of-view are introduced. For example, in an article on a new dry-cleaning process or controversial medical procedure, if points of view, pro and con are given reasonably equal treatment, then the resulting information will be more balanced and therefore reliable as to its role as support for decision making.

For example, in Chapter 3, the outlook for the climate and the impact this has on businesses built around winter sports was raised. Most reliable information on this topic will either quote points of view pro and con the continuation of the global warming trend or, if the article presents a single viewpoint, this will usually be acknowledged somewhere, either by the author or the editor.

If, however, the material is a profile of a company, a business person or an industry and only one or two sources, all from the same organization, are quoted, then the material may be suspect. It may even come closer to being "advertorial" material thinly disguised as a legitimate article but which has really been placed in the publication by the featured parties.

Spotting Disinformation

With Internet and Web sites, it is not always possible to check out who really put the information up and there are many bogus sites masquerading as the real thing. While it has always been important in information work to be able to spot the inaccurate and the out-of-date, it is even more important to spot the existence nowadays, especially in Web-based sources, of disinformation; information created with the deliberate intent of misleading and misinforming. One of the ways to spot such disinformation is when, plain and simple, it just doesn't make sense that the reported activities would be occurring. Another tip-off that the information might not be accurate is if it is presented in rather an emotional light; a Web site cast in such a tone may be the work of a disaffected ex-employee rather than the company whose name has been attached to this site.

Overall, if there is no corroboration in any other source for a piece of information, then it should be treated as highly suspect. If you read on the Internet, for example, that your competitor is putting up a new plant, you can turn to several other sources to see if this is the truth or a deliberate piece of disinformation. If no building permit has been issued in the locale where the building is supposed to be going up, then this is one indicator. If there is no actual physical construction going on, on the spot, that is another. If no construction suppliers have been hired or the job has not even been put out to tender, that is another indicator. If you cannot find any hiring notices in the paper for the staff needed at the new facility nor can you find any trucking company which recalls shipping the equipment needed into the site, that could well be another.

The perils of disinformation — or just being "snowed" by the sheer quantity of information on sources such as the Internet — are illustrated in the following example. A request made by a decision-maker to a subordinate to "get on the Web" and pull down all the articles on a new wonder drug could well produce references to several thousand documents or 'hits' from a great many sites. Taking this volume at face value, without further evaluation, could seriously jeopardize further decision making, if the company is a supplier to the pharmaceutical business, seeking new markets, or is a pharmaceutical company itself, trying to decide which avenues of R & D it needs to pull the plug on.

What is not immediately evident at the sheer quantity level, is how valid such items are or not. Ranking these documents as to likely importance won't help either, if the sources aren't carefully considered. An information novice might well report to their superior that they found 5,000 documents, saying how wonderful the new drug is and that the level of interest is high. An information specialist would take this a few steps further and identify that most of the documents originated with companies working on or selling the product. Such a specialist might then check other sources, such as news groups, which might contain feedback from those in clinical trials and non-Internet sources, such as trade journals, which have evaluated the pros and cons of the product. These viewpoints might be less glowing but allow for a more balanced report to be presented to the original requester. Of course, checking with other sources takes more time, really only a matter of 15 to 20 minutes, but takes away the charm of a source like the Internet, with its "instant pudding" seduction.

Correcting Poor Quality

Evaluation of sources may also indicate that, in spite of everyone's best efforts, the information obtained to support further decision making is actually of poor quality. Maybe the information is old; maybe there has been no updating of a source for five years, as can be the case nowadays, due to the problems of costs in publishing mentioned in Chapter 2. Maybe the information is incomplete; maybe data is only available for some of the markets or products under investigation, not the full range. It is possible to spend several days, if not weeks, in an information gathering exercise and still have an incomplete foundation for further decision making.

This is more likely to occur when sources tapped are just secondary sources; this is why most professional researchers undertake primary research as well — it is often the only way of "filling the gaps" and increasing the quality of available information. Therefore, the first step, when the information is being evaluated, is to see what type of sources have been used and, if there has been an over-reliance on secondary sources, supplement this with primary research.

The more experienced decision makers become with the information gathering process which supports their work, the more likely they will ask at this point: how many sources were used? Were the sources all that were available? Or could more have been found? This gets back to the tactic of "milking" sources discussed earlier; quite often a quality issue can be traced back to inadequate quantity of sources. In such cases, the ever present information overload and overwhelming number of sources may be scaring off a less experienced searcher.

However, if primary research has been conducted, and the resulting quality is poor, it will be necessary to examine the methodologies used and evaluate who was interviewed. Perhaps the population sampled was too small? Incorrectly selected? Perhaps too few experts were interviewed? In too narrow a range of industries?

Another culprit in the process can be the type of questions used. There are two main types of questions used in primary research: open-ended and closed. Closed questions tend to be those which can be answered by "Yes" or "No," by a monosyllabic answer "Once" "Twice," or by a number or rank. Which is fine, if this is the kind of information or answer sought. But if the desired results include an understanding of why a former customer switched to another supplier, why a competitor abandoned a market, why a supplier has decided to become a direct competitor, such cursory or shorthand responses won't do. For really in-depth information, open-ended questions are necessary and if they are not used, the quality of information will be lacking in the results.

Whatever the root cause of the problem, it may be necessary to conduct further research or broaden the base of sources used.

When Questions Lead to More Questions

Another reason why further research may be necessary before a decision can be made, is that the information raises as many questions as it answers. This is a development too few companies allow for in their decision making process.

Suppose you have been investigating why sales are down 25% in the Southwest and suppose the answer comes back that a new competitor or a new form of competition (such as a new technology or a major substitute) is the culprit, good decisions cannot be made until more is known. Who or what is the new competition? How long has it been around? How has it done in other markets? (Or is the Southwest the launch site; if so, what are the implications for our markets in other parts of the country?) The list of questions can be lengthy but the eventual decision will only be as good as the information obtained to answer them.

Selected References

"Market Research as a Way of Life Pays Off," *Silicon Valley News*, September 1997, p. 17.

Take a Coffee Break! It's Good For You, (Compilation) University of Winnipeg Press, Manitoba, 1998.

The Directory of Business Information Sources, Grey House Publishing, Lakeville CT, 1998, 1486 pp. Tel: 800/435-0868.

5 | Case By Case: Anatomy of Everyday Business Decisions

> *"Obviously, a man's judgement cannot be better*
> *than the information on which he has based it"*
> **Arthur Hays Sulzberger, 1948**

We've seen how the Seven Deadly Sins affect many business decisions and we've looked at information, what it is, how to find it, how to evaluate it. Now, it's time to put this into practice, to see how information can transform everyday business decisions and reduce the number of mistakes made.

What are the better ways to set about buying a company? To enter a market? What common mistakes with large capital purchases can be avoided with an input of information? What can be done to improve decisions made relative to competitors? Or to customers? While it is beyond the scope of this book to look at all the decisions made in business — as was explained in the preface, decisions about hiring and human resources have been deliberately omitted, as these are well discussed elsewhere — some of the more important decisions and particularly those which benefit the most from an input of external information, are discussed in this chapter.

There is also discussion, in each chapter, about who benefits the most from better decisions of the type under discussion along with what some of the payoffs are, both tangible and intangible. Another feature of these chapters is a checklist, suggesting some of the questions which need to be asked to guide information retrieval, research and analysis. Please note: *none* of these lists can be considered definitive. Just as some people, as discussed earlier, think there is some list of the Top Ten sources of information and that that's all they'll ever need to find it, there is a danger, in including the checklists, for some readers to think no further about their own questions. These lists are intended as a way to spark creativity, to stir the imagination, but they by no means represent the final word on research questions. Dare to ask your own as well!

Should We Buy This Company?

Expansion by way of acquisition is a frequent choice in the business world. Whether a company wishes to expand at home or abroad, buying another company to achieve this goal seems to make a lot of sense. Why, then, do so many acquisitions turn out less well than expected? Why do the costs of acquisition, especially with LBOs (Leveraged Buy-Outs), often nearly bury the acquirer, leading to a spate of downsizings and divestitures a few years later? Could it be that the company making the acquisition didn't ask the right questions? (Or committed one of the other Deadly Sins of decision making?)

How Acquisitions Happen

In theory, acquisitions are well-thought out business decisions, involving the best minds in a company or at external advisors, and follow a well-defined procedure. From the board level of the company comes the decision to proceed to see what companies might be available or which might be made available under the right inducements. This decision is relayed down the ranks where the company will assign staff to work on the project or, if the company uses an outside M & A (Mergers and Acquisitions) specialist, the directive goes to the external partner. (More on outside partners later).

There will likely be a lot of talk about "fit", about goals and about what the desired outcomes are. After this, the shopping begins in earnest, with the company thoroughly investigating available companies or companies which it would like to acquire. This is known as "due diligence." Then and only then does a recommendation or a short-list go back up to the decision makers who eventually make the wise and sound acquisition decision.

In reality, acquisitions rarely happen like this. When they are undertaken in-house, without use of an outside M & A specialist, they can be driven by ego and panic. In the case of publicly traded acquisition targets, when a company comes on the block, a feeding frenzy can be initiated as people scramble to bid for the company with only a limited due diligence process. In other scenarios, a decision is made to buy or target a particular acquisition candidate and then and only then is research done as a sort of back-stop measure, to back up what is really a "done deal." An extension of this scenario is when a decision is made that Company A has to acquire another company by a certain point in time — such as before the next board meeting — and a scramble then ensues to fill the gap.

Although external M & A specialists will swear up and down that their work is not undertaken in this manner, this is really a case of "smoke and mirrors." Most M & A specialists are paid as a percentage of the deals they do, which suggests that the pressure is always on to get the most money possible, not the best deal for the client, no matter how much such M & A firms go on about their own integrity. Then, too, they are equally under the same panic and ego pressures emanating from their clients to find something, quick. Add to this the fear that a "plum" might get away, and it is easy to see why acquisition decisions are often made in a very uninformed way.

What Gets Forgotten

One of the questions which is asked during most mergers and acquisitions is that about financials; most companies do give more than a cursory look at the target candidate's financial status but, unfortunately, most due diligence revolves around the numbers and is often exclusively devoted to them. The problem is, the numbers often lie.

One of the more frequently unasked questions — or group of questions — tied to an acquisition concerns the customers. Or, specifically, who are the customers? How will they view new ownership? Will they continue to buy from a new owner or will they walk? It is amazing that companies which expend full efforts on due diligence around the financials of an acquisition target never ask these key questions. They never seem to stop and say: what are we really buying here — a going concern or a piece of real estate (if that)? A thriving business will only stay that way if it still has customers. And there are few businesses nowadays where customers don't have choices about going elsewhere.

This may be particularly true if your company is in the same business already and is acquiring a competitor. Maybe the customers deal with the competitor because they don't like you! Maybe when the competitor is under new management (yours), the customers will leave in droves. This may sound like a simple issue, but if the purchaser is counting on the cash flow from the LBO to pay down debt, there is little or no margin for error. In spite of this, acquirers rarely are willing to invest in customer research — or, perhaps more importantly, lost customer research to find out why their ex-accounts left them — to round out their due diligence.

Another unasked question concerns markets and how sound these are. The question should always be asked: why is someone so willing to sell this business? What is really going on in the markets they serve? Once we own the target company, will we face a growing market or a declining one? In industries where the majority of companies are privately held, it is often difficult to get a true reading on the market outlook without a certain investment in research. Consider the example of the office coffee services company mentioned earlier. If they had not gone below the surface, and had stuck with the numbers covering population growth in Utah, they could have ended up with a real lemon on their hands in that state. The reason office coffee services operators were so keen to sell in Utah was that the business outlook was not particularly good. In the same exercise, it was found that Atlanta was also an equally bad market, even with the run up to the Olympic Games. There, the situation was compounded by over-entry of the field, meaning profitability was low at best. Market information showed the acquiring company to steer clear of acquisitions in these markets.

Another frequently unasked question in an acquisition scenario concerns the competitors. Suppose you are already in the industry and are planning to buy a competitor to consolidate and gain more market share with a view to market dominance? Before such a decision is even made, someone should ask questions about the likely responses of other competitors to such a move. Will they just sit tight and let you get on with your plans? Or will they respond in kind, by amalgamating themselves and forming an even bigger competitor to you, in spite of your newly acquired entity? Or, will competitors respond with a price war, cost cutting or some other tactic? Again, if the acquisition is to be paid for with cash flow from operations, any change in the overall dollar size of the industry and levels of cash flow revenue can seriously hamper the acquirer's ability to pay down debt. Yet, rarely do companies invest or invest enough in competitor research, prior to an acquisition, to round out their due diligence and really determine if the purchase will be a sound one.

Anatomy of an Ideal Acquisition

While the world may not be an ideal place, many acquisitions could approach the ideal — whether they proceed or not — if companies made a better use of available information as a tool in the decision making process. The first step in this procedure involves doing the unthinkable: spending money on gathering information which is not yet needed and may, in fact, never be needed, about competitors, customers, suppliers, and other entities. It would particularly involve investing money in tracking newly emerging companies and newly emerging technologies, whether or not the latter had posed a threat yet or not. Within this broad spectrum of information which has been gathered and organized and interpreted from the company's particular point of view (rather than relying on general analyses and discussions which are not from any company's particular point of view), opportunities could be evaluated within a broad spectrum of knowledge and activity.

This also suggests that spotting acquisition opportunities would start to come from lower down the organization and move up the chain rather than being top-down driven, which is why so many which occurred in the latter part of the 20th century did not work out very well. While some companies have reorganized themselves to be more bottom-up driven and closer to the customer, it will probably be some time before they can make the leap to allowing more junior staff and front-line workers to have this kind of input into acquisition opportunities but it is a change that will be necessary in the 21st century.

As potential acquisition candidates emerge from this broad spectrum of information and within the company's particular operating environment as to which opportunities would enhance its business, further investment in information is required to thoroughly analyze all aspects of the potential acquisition, such as: customers, lost customers, prospective customers, markets and the overall industry in which the target operates, especially if it is in a different industry to the acquiring company's. It also would not hurt, at this point, to take another hard look at potential offshore competition which could move into the domestic market and to thoroughly scout out new technologies which could sideswipe the industry and totally displace both the acquirer and acquiree at some point in the future. With this kind of grass roots movement in place, steps could then be taken to move the decision making further up the chain and involve those who actually approve the purchase.

What to Look For

The role of thorough and extensive information in making, or avoiding, an acquisition can be illustrated by the case of a major airline which, a few years ago, had its eye on a small but very high profile commuter airline. Rather than look at just the financial information — a task somewhat complicated by the fact the commuter airline was privately held and no overtures had yet been made which would have opened the books — the airline commissioned research to investigate the target commuter airline. This involved extensive searches, one of which turned up the fact that just about every plane the commuter airline supposedly owned was in hock, deep hock in fact. The airline really owned nothing and was seriously in debt. On this basis, the acquiring airline decided to turn its attention elsewhere.

Information can also give the green light, as was the case a few years ago when Woolworth's was interested in expanding by acquiring smaller, regional department stores. The company had its eye on one in Newfoundland, a chain of maybe four or five stores strategically located around the province. Since this small chain was privately held, there were no securities exchange-type documents to provide the financials or other data. There were also a lot of unanswered questions nagging the decision makers at Woolworth's: was this chain profitable? Had it any plans for expansion or renovation which might place a burden on its cashflow? What was management like? The company was essentially interested, in a case like this, for points of leverage to use in any negotiations.

Where the Information Came From

What is interesting in both these cases is that the information did not turn up in material supplied by the target companies — which actually supplied nothing that revealing, since they knew nothing about a possible takeover — but came from public domain sources. In many acquisitions situations, since the potential target is a cooperating party, the acquirer simply looks at financial data supplied by the target, numbers which should always be considered suspect, given their source. Research about the commuter airline not only gathered up press coverage from newspapers and business magazines (this example pre-dates the Internet) along with material supplied by the company itself, but also tapped public records, such as incorporation papers, credit reports and registers of leased property. It was this last item that proved most valuable; it provided a detailed list of aircraft, some of which had been financed and then refinanced.

As for the Newfoundland department store chain, tapping several public sources of data produced a foundation of information: municipal tax records confirmed size of stores plus tax rates, directories gave headcounts per store, advertisements fleshed out details of merchandise, while the occasional article from the local press provided background on managers. But, in this case, the "glue" which pulled the information together and answered the key questions came from interviews with store managers and head office personnel.

Information to support the acquisition strategy of the office coffee services company discussed earlier also came from a range of sources, many of them also in the public domain. One of the starting points was actually Yellow Pages ads, which include a wealth of detail over and above basic company name, address, phone number and line of business. The scope of each company's service, "extras" they provided, details about territories served and any franchise affiliations also came to light this way. This data was supplemented with searches of databases, such as Dun & Bradstreet databases, searches of government filings, for incorporation papers, plus scans of trade magazines for articles and more ads.

The next step in the process was to turn to industry associations, many of which provided directories of their members and other background. All of which was further supplemented with product literature from the target companies. In the case of chains or franchises, interviews were also conducted with head office personnel.

Even then, this abundance of information only answered some of the client's questions or simply corroborated what was already known; further details were obtained by conducting interviews, at the grass roots level, with the operators themselves.

What Is The Payoff From Better Acquisition Decisions?

The payoff from better acquisition decisions can usually be measured by dollars saved instead of swallowed by the costs of servicing a debt or otherwise reducing the company's war-chest for what might be better opportunities which come along, as was the case for the airline interested in expanding.

In the case of Woolworth's, a better informed decision, at a better price, could be made, because both the strong and weak points of the acquisition target were known and negotiations could proceed accordingly.

The benefits from making better acquisition — or merger — decisions can be felt all along the chain: from employees to customers to shareholders. Given that statistics show that only a small percentage of mergers or acquisitions add shareholder value — in fact, 65 to 75% of mergers *destroy* shareholder value — whether the owners of a company are a few owner-managers or whether they are a sizeable number of members of the public at large, better decisions about whether to buy a company or not will benefit all of them.

Beyond this, employees at both companies will benefit if perhaps fewer of the ego-driven mergers and acquisitions occur. One of the main saboteurs of a successful acquisition is corporate culture; few executives seem to have yet developed the knack of blending two organizations which are not just separated by geographic location, lines of business, and customer bases, but also by corporate culture, suggesting another question or two which needs to be asked before any overtures are ever made: How similar or dissimilar are the corporate cultures of the two entities? How do they do business? How do their employees go about their tasks? What do their offices look like? What does it feel like to work over there?

There are cases where not making an acquisition — or merging — might be the wiser decision to make, meaning a company could therefore avoid the sizeable costs of disruption to its business, not to mention the price tag of severance pay, by deciding to pass. There are other ways to invest in the business and grow, as long as decision makers can get off the "acquisitions hobby-horse" and look elsewhere.

Who Benefits?

Customers will also benefit from wiser, more well-thought out corporate mergers. One of the consequences of many an acquisition or merger is reduced facilities to serve customers (as occurs with many bank mergers), reduced product lines (if the acquired company's best seller was a competitive threat to the acquirer's "lesser light," it is not a given the best seller will remain on the market. Old Demon Ego stalks the post-acquisition decision maker) and reduces service (many newly blended corporate entities are beset by confusion over who does what; a "business as usual" environment is very rare).

Checklist   5.1

Questions about the target

- How similar or dissimilar are the corporate cultures of our two entities?
- How does the target do business?

- How do their employees go about their tasks?
- What does their facility look like?
- What does it feel like to work over there?
- How long have the employees been with the company?
- Are the employees adaptable or change-resistant?
- How many of the existing management is at or near retirement?
- What assumptions do we hold about this target?
- How many of them are accurate?
- Will they be willing to sell happily?
- Why do they want to sell right now?
- Is this really an opportunity?

Questions about the customers

- Who are the customers of the target?
- How much overlap is there, with our customer base?
- How will their customers view new ownership?
- Will they continue to buy from a new owner or will they go elsewhere?
- Why do they buy from the target now?
- What products, services, benefits and features will we have to retain to keep the customers?

Questions about the competition

- Who are the competitors to the target?
- Are they the same as our competitors or are they unknown entities?
- What defensive or offensive measures will the competitors take in response to our acquisition?
- Which of the competitors might amalgamate in response?
- What other tactics or initiatives might they employ to outflank us?
- Which of the competitors might be able to control the agenda in the industry in spite of our acquisition?
- What level of alternate or substitute competition exists to the product/ service we are acquiring?

Questions about the market

- Is the market our target serves growing or shrinking?
- What is the long-term market outlook?
- What market forces, such as demographics, government regulation, supplier shifts, etc., could dramatically affect the future we face?
- How sizeable is the potential market in other geographic areas?

Or Shall We Sell A Division?

The usual reason given for a company selling a division or subsidiary is a lack of "fit." Management decides that the company must get back to its "core businesses" so anything not defined as core is vulnerable to the axe. Ironically, some of the candidates for divestiture are often those companies or entities acquired during poor acquisition decisions, as discussed in the previous chapter.

The result is often short-term gain for long-term pain. Before a decision is made to sell a division, branch, subsidiary or any other part of an overall enterprise, there needs to be considerable attention paid to the decision and the information used to support it.

How Divestitures Happen

In theory, divestitures happen when a company realizes that it does not have the expertise to run a particular part of its business or that certain parts of the company's holdings are taking resources away from the more profitable activities. Or, the company decides it wants to reprioritize where it reinvests in its activities. After considerable deep reflection, and with a great deal of sadness, the announcement is made that it is time to go separate ways and so part of the business will be sold. The selling company then sets out to canvas the market for prospective buyers who will be a good "parent" for the sold entity, sort of like an adoption process. This way, both the staff and customers of the divested entity will be well taken care of.

In reality, many divestitures occur in a climate of fear and panic or are driven by ego. Someone realizes that second or third quarter profits will be down and so a quick fix to stem losses is sought out. Another driver of divestitures can be the desire to protect executive bonuses meaning the less profitable parts of the company or less interesting parts have to be sold off. Charlie, the Executive VP, may decide he is tired of flying to Peoria or Albuquerque or — worse — Kinshasa or Matto Grosso once a month. Part of the business has become a serious irritation, so it's got to go. Under these circumstances, steps are taken, to amputate, to get the gangrene out fast.

The rationality brought to the divestiture decision can also be distorted by use of an external M & A specialist, one which has been approached, in this case, to "shop" the entity for sale and find a buyer. While there are undoubtedly M & A specialists who concern themselves with "fit" and with finding "win-win" situations for all parties, given that the fees of such specialists are usually a percentage of the deal, there is obviously a temptation to get the best monetary deal, not make the best decision. Then, such specialists are often given rather narrow timeframes in how they "shop" the deal: a shortlist of candidates in 3 weeks, concluded negotiations in another month — such might be the rather frantic mandate provided.

What Gets Forgotten

These panic-stricken scenarios come up because many decision makers have too narrow a time horizon. Suppose, for example, that a beer company also part-owns a sports franchise (such as a baseball team) and a broadcast channel dedicated to sports. And, under the direction of a new parent overseas, comes the decision that running a team or being in broadcasting are not "core businesses", since the core business is strictly beer-making. So the team and the TV station have to go.

Such decision making is wrong because it is made in a vacuum. Before the amputation occurs, someone needs to look at how the parts contribute to the whole. A whole slew of questions needs to be asked to come up with accurate answers. If other beer makers, for example, are maintaining links to sports teams and broadcast outlets, will the company be at a disadvantage if it doesn't maintain such entities as well? How do the profiles of the team and/or the broadcast channel feed demand for the core product, beer? How will the customers view the change? Will they still buy the product if the owner of the team makes a competing product?

Not obtaining information to answer such questions jeopardizes the success of the eventual decision made. And since at first, everything goes well after the dismemberment (attributable to the fact the momentum built up while the parts were working together carries over), the real result of the decision doesn't show up until sometime later. And, by then, it is usually too late to reverse the damage.

Another frequently unasked question when companies are considering a divestiture is: if we wanted to get back in at some future point, what will the costs be? And will there be anything to buy? It is not unheard of for a company, in the throes of financial difficulties, to sell a prized division or subsidiary, only to regret it a few years later and want to purchase it back, especially if this will give the entré to re-entering a market seen as having a lot of potential. Unfortunately, the sold division or subsidiary may not be on the market, may not exist in a form which could be acquired, or just may be unavailable for some other reason. In such cases, this will either lead the former divestor to make a poor acquisition decision, such as bidding an inflated price to recapture the divested entity, or it will buy a substitute that proves to be less valuable. Since many divestiture decisions are based on immediate money needs, such as improving short-term profitability, very rarely does anyone spend the time or money gathering information to look far enough down the road to see if selling is also going to be a wise decision.

Another question which is often left unasked during divestitures is: if a competitor buys this division or subsidiary, how will this change the competitive landscape? Will it put our company at an even further disadvantage? Since a divestiture of one part of the company cannot be divorced entirely from its impact on other parts, it is important to invest the time and money gathering information to fully study this issue. Although the business with the for sale sign on it may be seen as non-core, if it has any relationship to other, more core parts of the business, allowing a competitor to get this close may be detrimental to all the other parts of the business.

This kind of situation is frequently found in the banking industry, where bankers gnash their teeth about the inconvenience of providing transaction services, such as checking accounts, which often don't contribute to the bottom line. Such products may, however, often be "loss leaders" encouraging both individuals and corporate accounts to bring sizeable pieces of business to the bank: mortgages, credit lines, pension plans, etc.

Investigation of such issues will allow a company to see if it perhaps should single out another part of its enterprise for sale — if raising cash quickly is a serious concern — or to look at ways to somehow hang onto the division, branch, or subsidiary under consideration for sale.

It is equally important to ask how things will turn out if a non-competitor buys the entity which is for sale. What will be the impact on the industry of letting a new company in to become a possible competitor? What will be the impact on the selling company? Although the repercussions from admitting a new player into the industry can be quite severe, few, if any, companies currently bother to invest in gathering information to probe these issues fully.

When they do bother to find out some key pieces of information, decision making becomes easier. A major aluminum producer, in the throes of rationalizing its business, decided to sell its building products division as being neither a major contributor to profits nor a good fit with the core business. Rather than just announce that the division was for sale, the company's Controller decided to find out more about the competitors who might be candidates to buy.

This involved learning more about the scope of operations of each competitor, where they were located, their key customers, weak spots in terms of markets and customer base, financial resources and more. Once the information was in hand, the Controller was able to "cherry-pick" a purchase candidate and package the entity for sale to make it seem irresistible. As a result, the divestiture happened quickly, at relatively low cost to the selling and buying entities and without a lot of public fanfare (which had been one of the objectives). The information to support this smooth transition was largely readily available in the public domain.

Anatomy of an Ideal Divestiture

While making the mind-shift to gathering and using information — even if there is no immediate application for it — is a shift few companies have yet made (but most will have to make in the 21st century), in an ideal scenario, information would be gathered and analyzed to develop a range of scenarios around possible future divestitures. Such information, brought into the company on an ongoing basis, would allow for hypothesizing scenarios based on the growth, stagnation or decline of all key parts of an organization's business. And projecting how these futures would look will allow companies to determine ahead of time, which parts of the business they would keep, which they would part own and seek out joint venture partners for and which they would sell off, long before an actual decision has to be made. Information could then be gathered to keep a database of potential acquirers, companies which could provide the necessary purchases for the divested entity but which would not produce any harm to the parts of the business remaining.

Again, this requires more bottom-up participation in decision making rather than top-down driven decision making, a leap most companies are not yet ready to make. Another complicating factor is that, in a divestiture, key, front-line employees, are asked to decide that parts of the business have to be sold when it is their own jobs that will be lost. Making the transition to such objective pragmatism is not easy to achieve.

What to Look For

The example cited earlier in this book of a large chemical company deciding to divest its sulfuric acid technology business illustrates what gets forgotten or, conversely, what needs to be more closely examined. What the managers who purchased the business should have looked more closely at, to save themselves some pain, is the factors which had led a large, successful parent with deep pockets to not be able to keep pace with others in the industry. What were the magical ingredients — the chemistry (pardon the pun) — that had made others successful, especially firms that were actually smaller than the divesting parties?

Some of the success could be attributed to employee ownership at the competing entities but this was not the only factor, one which the managers would soon come to replicate themselves. Another was focus; although the competing entities had more than one line of business, such lines were all much closer to the core business and there was greater "synergy" as it's known. Other factors included locations; a physical presence in Europe and Asia seemed to offer some advantage while a higher profile among customers contributed. Then, there was an issue of timing; in terms of business development and innovation, the competing companies were just that much further ahead on the "learning curve".

In the case of the building products company, the key information which was pivotal to success concerned prospective buyers' weaknesses and spotting ways in which the entity for sale would strengthen the acquirer's overall operations.

Where the Information Came From

In the sulfuric acid case, the information which showed up all these things — and suggested an LBO by a group of managers was not such a good idea — came readily to hand. Corporate brochures, while they do tend to be self-congratulatory in nature, contain a factual basis. Such corporate literature plus incorporation papers and regulatory filings confirmed the scope of operations for each of the companies and where they were located.

The level of employee ownership and commitment also came through from such sources plus articles and profiles published by independent sources about the companies. Lines of business could also be determined from such sources and also published announcements of project awards. Last but not least, there were the customers, past and present, who happily discussed why they chose these firms to work with.

Some of the insight the managers should have heeded therefore came from direct statements of fact while other understanding should have come from "reading between the lines" in the customer comments. Either way, the information was reasonably readily available and just required an input of time and effort to retrieve it.

For the Controller at the building products company, the information to pin down who the best purchaser would be came from both public domain and private (interview) sources. Most companies which are privately held do not realize just how much material is in the public domain; in this case, tax roll information, details about leased property, credit reports and sales projections all popped up in public sources. Interviews with customers, suppliers and the target companies rounded out the search.

What is the Payoff from Better Divestiture Decisions?

One of the more obvious payoffs from better divestiture decisions is fewer costs from selling off the wrong parts of the business; in larger entities, the sum of the parts usually is greater than the whole. Reckless dismemberment can weaken the future of the body which remains after the amputation. Companies do sometimes come to this conclusion in the nick of time; the beer company mentioned earlier decided, at the last minute, not to sell its stake in the sports team. Someone was able to persuade the European owners of the realities of marketing beer in North America.

Better divestiture decisions also benefit both seller and buyer financially, provided the buyer is also making well-informed acquisition decisions. In such cases, the divestiture can be likened to a successful arranged marriage; the seller ends up with a more streamlined business, easier to run, plus cash from the sale while the buyer adds a logical extension to its business.

Who Benefits?

Employees are one of the earlier beneficiaries of better divestiture decisions, as the company for which they work is more likely to be kept as a going concern if the purchaser has been well chosen. They can also benefit if their area of activity had been something of an "orphan" before and now has a family. For the aluminum company, building products had been a very small part of its business and one on which it had focussed only minimal attention. Once acquired, the employees found themselves part of a larger entity whose sole focus was building products, which was a plus. More resources could be devoted to them; there were more opportunities for training and advancement.

For executives and managers, a better divestiture decision can mean not having "egg on their faces" a few years down the road when someone, such as a board member, starts asking why the division or subsidiary was sold off when the market for the product or service is now so hot? At the same time, getting rid of parts of the company which it really doesn't make sense to keep, frees up both financial and human resources to devote to more profitable aspects of the company or those which offer greater long term potential.

Checklist   5.2

Questions about prospective purchasers

- Who might be available to purchase and how does our division fit with what they're doing now?
- Would the division add new customers or overlap those they already have?
- Does the product or service duplicate what they do or does it line extend?
- Do the best candidates have the financial resources to take this on?
- Are they geographically close to where the division is or are there logistics and other management issues to resolve?

Questions about the customers

- How will our customers view the sale?
- What will be the impact on integrated sales? If they buy a series of products and services from us, what will be the impact on our overall business?
- Will we lose customers from other parts of our business over this sale?

Questions about competitors

- If a competitor buys this business, how will this affect our competitive position in other markets?
- If a competitor does acquire the business, will this provide them with leverage to win away customers from other areas of our business?

Questions about re-entry

- If we want to get back into this business in the future, will we be able to?
- What will the costs be?
- Will there be such a business or distinct entity available for purchase?
- If no entities exist which we can buy, what will the costs be for starting from scratch?
- Will we be able to afford this?
- How long would it take, from start-up, to get something up and running?

Questions about ourselves

- What options exist other than a divestiture?
- Have we fully explored all options?
- If we solved our short-term problems some other way, would we still want to sell?
- What needs does selling really meet?

Is This a Market to Enter?

Much money and effort can be expended to enter new markets; whether the market is at home or abroad, the cost of starting from scratch and building up a business in what is often unfamiliar territory can be very high. Such factors alone suggest that any company thinking about entering a new market should think twice and gather sufficient information on which to base the decision.

How Market Entries Happen

In theory, the decision to enter a new market is a well-reasoned and well-informed exercise. The company identifies a need for new markets for existing products because such markets are needed for further growth. This conclusion has been reached after much consideration of current markets which have either reached saturation or are close to it. This realization leads to a lot of further analysis as the company identifies the key variables which must be present in a new market in order for success to occur. The nature of the market, economic conditions, growth rates, the nature of the population, socio-economic indicators, affluence or earnings indicators, are all thoroughly considered and a profile of the ideal market for expansion determined. The company then sets about identifying a match and once one is found, systematically plans to enter it. Staff are sent down to the market to "suss it out" at the grass roots level. How best can the company achieve market entry? Should it set up locally or look for distributors or other local partners? Who will staff the venture? Who will sell the products? Only when these and other questions have been fully explored does the market entry occur.

In reality, rarely is a market entry decision made in such a well-informed manner. Sales are found to be flat and so the company decides to pounce quickly, where it can boost its numbers. India and China have large populations, surely there are masses of consumers there waiting to buy our products? Or, domestically, don't people say that the Southwest is growing very rapidly, booming in fact? Let's go there. Or — a frequent temptation for U.S. companies — what about Canada? It's close by. The fact that, although there are huge numbers of people, the consumers in India and China are not ready for the product doesn't enter anyone's thinking. The fact the Southwest is growing but the climate there is so unsuited to the company's top-of-the-line snow blowers remains unrecognized. And no one stops to consider that Canada is a very small market, with horrible distribution logistics. Market entry therefore becomes an act of desperation rather than one of deliberation.

What Gets Forgotten

This was the sort of phenomenon which gripped a number of companies a few years ago when they heard that others were entering the Mexican market, spurred on by the promise of free trade under NAFTA. The advantages of a *maquiladora* sounded sweet. Everyone wanted one, much the way small children decide they want a tamagotchi or whatever the latest toy is. Instead of being a rational decision, based on a factual assessment of the opportunity — if there even is one — such market entries are "me-too" endeavors, examples of "If it works for them..." decision making. In the case of companies deciding to enter a foreign market, such as Mexico, a great many questions need to be asked and a great deal of information gathered. Not the least of these questions, if a competitor's initiative is the spur to the decision, is: Why are they entering this market? Is it part of a planned expansion? Or is it driven by some negative factor, such as a cost-cutting move? Or is it a defensive measure?

Asking these sorts of questions will soon point the direction to answers which will show whether it's worth going further or not. If the Mexico market is indeed expanding rapidly, there is increasing demand for your product but no local sources of supply, for example, then it may indicate an opportunity. But if the answers indicate your competitor is "turning tail" and running to Mexico for other reasons, it may be better to wait and see what the future holds.

Another question which is often unasked but needs to be, especially for overseas market entries, is: What hidden factors could derail profitability? Even in domestic markets, there may be unseen factors, such as taxes, the political environment, or hostility to outsiders, as happened in the case of Canadian Tire's expansion into Texas, which will make the market entry extremely difficult, even when the numbers suggest a lot of potential is there.

Another question to ask, especially when the new market seems like virgin territory, is: Why hasn't anyone else done this? If an opportunity to enlarge your business in a new market really exists, chances are other companies will have identified it, including your competitors. Identifying a growing market area in terms of the broad numbers, but where no visible competition exists, is not a good sign that you have found a license to print money.

This should have occurred to the guiding spirits behind Koo Koo Roo and should have prompted the search for answers, long before ambitious expansion plans were announced. They had spotted a "void in the market" namely, no chain supplying fast-food chicken to the upscale segment. Perhaps this segment does not really exist in the chicken business? Or only exists in some markets, such as California? Perhaps upscale consumers find chicken easy to prepare at home and seek something else when they dine out? If there really was a nationwide segment of upscale consumers looking for a healthy, reasonably priced chicken dinner, it is a fair guess to say the other chicken chains would have filled it long ago.

Alternatively, maybe the market among the upscale segment is small and can quickly reach saturation, as with El Pollo Loco. Maybe there isn't room for another chain? The loss, by Kenny Rogers Roasters, of 200 restaurants in

4 years and the company's subsequent seeking of bankruptcy protection, suggests this might be the case. Information to answer such questions or at least reduce the number of questions is readily available in a range of secondary and primary sources and could have been tapped.

The non-existence of competition should set off a lot of warning bells and indicate that time must be spent on gathering information to find out why other companies are avoiding the area. Some companies discovered this the hard way, when, for example, they decided to enter the newly emerging Russian market. Not factoring in an issue such as organized crime which is a way of life there can seriously impair the assessment of the potential in the market. Alternatively, if a company still decides to go ahead under these circumstances, knowing the problem exists at least allows for development of strategies to deal with it.

One can only speculate what the eventual outcome will be as city after city tries to enter the gambling business and set up a casino. If ever there was an example of All Aboard the Bandwagon decision making, this is it! Once there was just Las Vegas for legal gambling in the United States, then Atlantic City got in on the act. Then various First Nations decided to set up a casino on the reserve. Now, just about any city or region with a depressed economy sees casino gambling as a nirvana for economic revitalization.

As a quick glance at Europe and other jurisdictions can show, it is not beneficial, in the long run, to set up casinos on every street corner. There's Monte Carlo and some licensed gambling clubs in London but, by and large, little else available in Europe. In the Far East, there's Macao but even nearby entrepreneurial Hong Kong has avoided jumping on the casino bandwagon.

This suggests gambling may be a market made more successful by under-entry of the field not over-entry. Many cities which rush headlong into this could well find the decision was a bad one when, a few years down the road, revenues are flat and the social costs of gambling are beyond the means of the public purse to solve.

Anatomy of an Ideal Market Entry

Whether a company is planning to enter a market by simply selling its products there or plans to set up shop physically, the information to be gathered to make such decisions sound follows a familiar pattern. Again, it involves investing in information before you actually need to have it and in the possibility that it will not all be needed. In the case of domestic markets, information on all the parts of the country in which you do not yet have a presence, should be gathered in their entirety: economic situation, growth rate, population growth, business formation rates, housing starts, all of which is readily available in the public domain. With non-domestic markets, similar information can also be gathered for the most likely candidates, such as countries with rapidly developing economies or others which are stabilizing following periods of political unrest.

To whatever information is gathered from public domain sources, at some point, visiting the place in-person or, at least, having someone based in the area gather further information to answer specific questions, is a necessary step. All this information has to, of course, be organized and then sifted and analyzed in the light of newer developments which occur. Maybe the population of a particular target area is growing but if economic uncertainty or some sort of political instability is clouding the picture, then this area falls lower in priority as far as market entry is concerned. At this stage, it's also a good idea to identify other non-competing companies who are already in the market, to tap into their experiences and learn at the grass roots level what it is really like there. Once again, such decision making will be as much bottom-up as it is top-down; input, for example, from customer service order-takers who notice a high number of orders coming in from an area where the company does not have a real market presence, can be a nice way of validating initiatives which are being thought of by other people at the company.

With overseas markets, it's also important to gather plenty of information ahead of time about cultural, religious or ethnic taboos which would make marketing there difficult. In some cases, these factors will forever close the market to you, regardless of any government policy about foreigners entering the market. But much better to find this sort of information out ahead of time rather than try to sell a product for which the color has negative connotations or is culturally inappropriate.

What to Look For

Of course, when available information suggests the new market initiative is not a good idea, it is best to pay attention, something the major consumer goods company, with its eye on the dental supplies business failed to do.

In this case, the company sabotaged itself, before it got started, by asking not necessarily the wrong questions but only some of the questions. Before detailed research was undertaken, the company had determined drill bits were a low-cost item to produce, ideal for a market entry. No doubt the thinking went; we'll enter the market at the lowest possible cost point and build up from there.

The questions which didn't get asked soon enough, those which indicate what the company should have been looking for were: Why are drill bits so cheap to produce? What does this do to the perceived value of the product among purchasers? If they are so cheap to produce what does this do to their profit potential? Why are there still so many producers or suppliers? And what role do drill bits play, both in the dentist's business and in our potential competitors' business?

Asking questions like these — and others — sometimes indicates a market is premature or your idea is ahead of its time. A company interested in offering its LAN (Local Area Network) expertise on an outsourcing basis, discovered that the market just wasn't there yet. While people had made the move to outsourcing data centers and batch operations, many were still wary about this practice and were not ready to outsource areas of business perceived as more sensitive, such as networks.

Prior to undertaking research, however, this company had recognized a need to probe the pros and cons of its plan, before making any decision. This saved them the considerable costs they would have incurred, if they had gone ahead on an uninformed basis, not to mention potential embarrassment, had they done so and fallen flat.

Where the Information Came From

In this case, the information which raised red flags and suggested postponing the decision came from other outsourcing providers (who were approached discreetly, so as not to "let the cat out of the bag") and from customers and prospective customers. Since this work was undertaken in the early days of LANs, companies which already had networks as well as those considering one were canvassed. The information therefore came largely from the primary research interviewing referenced in Chapter 4; as with so many key business decisions, secondary sources, for all their abundance, could not be tapped, simply because, on this topic, they were non-existent.

The same was actually true for the information about the dental supplies business; as discussed earlier, a mix of articles, product catalogs, price lists, a visit to a trade show and mainly primary interviews yielded the answers.

But none of these sources on their own gave the complete picture; it was tapping them sequentially plus the cumulative impact of the information gathered which provided the support needed to make further decisions. (That the decision makers chose to ignore the facts is not a reflection of the information or its availability.)

As for Koo Koo Roo, one of the key tactics, early on, should have been to ask successful competitors why they had not developed a nationwide concept to serve the upscale market? Or, in the case where competitors had done so, how large did they see the segment as? What was the ceiling on growth potential?

Some people might laugh and say no competitor will tell you this or, that any competitor so approached would provide disinformation to "throw you off the trail." This is not actually true; it all depends on how you ask the question. Well-thought out questions in the hands of a skillful interviewer would likely have yielded many of the answers sought. Those not provided directly could have been obtained by "reading between the lines." From this base of insight, Koo Koo Roo could have turned to other publicly available data, such as demographics and socio-economics, along with projections, to see what the real potential for their concept was. Further research about regional food preferences and consumer concepts of what is "healthy" would have helped refine the overall plan for the company.

What is the Payoff from Better Market Entry Decisions?

Whether the market entered is at home or abroad, one of the more obvious payoffs from making better market entry decisions is that the company will still be seen as a winner in the eyes of employees, competitors, suppliers, shareholders, and others.

While it may be possible to buy or sell a company quietly, deciding to enter China or South America is a very public and noticeable decision, which, if it proves to be a bad decision, also attracts a lot of attention. Both of Canadian Tire's forays into the U.S. market were high profile, as were its market exits. Questions immediately arose about the competence of current managers. Executive control of the organization has subsequently changed hands several times.

In financial terms, the payoff from picking markets for expansion on a more informed basis is obviously fewer losses from unwise choices and greater profitability from the "good picks."

Who Benefits?

Most parties benefit from better market entry decisions. For employees, there is greater scope for new challenges and advancement. Shareholders benefit in seeing their stocks rise in value. Customers benefit as both new customers are able to enjoy products and services otherwise unavailable to them while existing customers have their choice of supplier "validated" in that the company is obviously a winner. Suppliers benefit due to expanded demand for their services.

Checklist	**5.3**

Questions about markets

- Why do we need to enter a new market? Have we fully explored opportunities in existing markets?
- Which of our products could be adapted to increase sales in existing markets?
- If we must enter a new market, should this be at home or abroad?
- Which market has the optimum conditions for a market entry?
- What factors, such as crime, economic conditions, government regulations, cultural values, etc., would slow down or inhibit our progress?
- Which non-competitor companies already in that market can we turn to for insight and advice?

Questions about strategy and operations

- How can we best achieve market entry?
- Should we set up locally or look for a distributor or partner already in the market?
- Which of our current team is best suited to running this activity?
- What is a realistic timetable to get things up and running from scratch?
- What will the start-up costs be?
- What will the ongoing costs be?
- Can we replicate our entire modus operandi in the new market or do we have to invent structures and procedures to suit local conditions?

Questions about products/services

- Which of our products will be the best choice for our first offering?
- Do consumers in the target market already use a similar product or is it new?

- If it is new, what level of acceptance will there be?
- What sort of awareness will we have to build?
- If the product is available but little used, why is this?

Questions about competitors

- Which of our competitors is already in this market?
- If they aren't there, why not?
- If they are, what prompted them to enter it?
- Are they committed to the market long-term or is it just a passing fancy?
- If no one else in our industry has looked at this market, why not?
- Which of our competitors has been in this market and exited?
- If so, why did they leave?
- What new competitors, especially companies we've never heard of, will we now compete against?

Should We Stay Or Should We Go? Market Exits Need Research, Too

Deciding to get out of a market is no less important than the decision to enter it in the first place, but such decisions are equally often made on the basis of emotion and not on the basis of rational inquiry. The way companies select markets to exit often parallels the way they decide on how to divest divisions, subsidiaries or branches. Very rarely are these decisions well-informed.

How Exit Decisions Happen

In theory, market exit decisions are made after careful analysis of a full spectrum of information and detailed deliberation of the implications of leaving a particular spot. Before the decision is made to pull out of India or Illinois, as the case may be, a range of scenarios are developed as to how business might look three, five, ten years down the road and only when no possibility of real success has been determined, does the company pull the plug. An equally important part of this process is looking at scenarios which are on both sides of the decision: staying and leaving. Such companies always fully assess that they will not want to get back into the market, once they have left.

In reality, many market exits are based on short-term and uninformed thinking. Rarely are they made in the context of the long-term interests of customers, employees or shareholders. Consider how the Vice President of a large nationwide jewelry chain charged an independent research company with an assignment relative to a possible market exit a few years ago. "Find me everything you can about the Calgary market and make it look as bad as possible," he advised. Regardless of how the market really was in this city, he wanted to know all the negatives, indicators of economic downturn, level of exits by other companies, declines in per capita income, etc. This was information he would be presenting to his board of directors, many of whom would not be advised of the real reasons for his desire to exit this market, namely, he was tired of flying there. (This was back in the days before frequent flyer points became so widely available). Did the company make a wise decision when they did exit the market? Today, Alberta has one of the stronger economies in Canada and had the company looked this far ahead, they may have been able to pick up on signs that exiting the Calgary market was an undesirable strategy and ways should be found to stay there for the long haul.

What Gets Forgotten

Although many senior executives at companies are career employees and stay with the company for ten, fifteen, sometimes twenty or more years, they tend to exhibit very short term thinking. All it may take is a couple of years of poor results and they want to pull the plug. Why should we stay in the Minneapolis market, they say, when we're losing money? However, before decisions are made to exit any market, particular questions need to be asked: Why are we in the Minneapolis market? What led, however long ago, to the decision to enter it? If those contributing factors made sense then, do they still make sense now? What has changed in Minneapolis to put an exit decision on our agenda? Asking such questions of course points to the need for information to answer them and that is why it is always easier — but not better — to avoid asking the questions in the first place. It may require extensive research to get at some of the underlying issues: If the Minneapolis market was entered fifty or more years ago, then the people who were in on the decision may no longer be with the company. They may not even be alive! Finding the answers may be time-consuming.

And, if patterns hold true, the answers will themselves raise more questions and the need for more information. If Minneapolis was a good market for fifty years, what went wrong? Was it external factors? Or internal? The mere mention of internal factors immediately raises the specter of blame and finger-pointing; no wonder then, that many exit decisions are made with a

Fly by the Seat of Your Pants methodology, which is so much more ego-soothing than the rigors of a real investigation.

Even a casual observer of corporate behavior must wonder how the decision to exit all markets was made by such a long-established store as Woolworth's. When the company announced it was not just exiting selected markets but all markets and was dropping use of the Woolworth's banner, shock waves were sent through a number of communities, both among employees and customers. While some store locations were undoubtedly unprofitable, this was not the case in all of them; in some city centers or smaller communities, Woolworth's was the only store or one of the few stores of any size.

Did the decision makers ever bother to consider the chain store-by-store? If some of the stores were profitable, why weren't these kept? Could not the profitable stores have been sold as a scaled-down chain or perhaps franchised (since Woolworth's did not want to keep the banner)? The company's decision to exit the general merchandise-department store category at a time when the one-stop shopping convenience of department stores is regaining popularity with consumers is also somewhat surprising. The company has instead chosen to focus on its athletic footwear and specialty chains, at a time when these lines of business are encountering some bumps in the road. All of which suggests behind-the-scenes decision making made in something of an information vacuum, perhaps prompted by Old Demon Ego, with more than a *soupçon* of some of the other deadly sins.

Another question that is often avoided with market exits is: If we do exit, and circumstances change, can we easily get back in? Given that economies, whether local, regional or national, tended to be cyclical, when things look bad and people leave, they very rarely consider what the picture will look like when the economy is on the upswing. During bad times, real estate and other resources may be available at fire-sale prices; when things are booming, rents and other costs sky rocket. This has been shown in a variety of markets, including cities in newly emerging markets such as Russia and China. Sometimes it might be better to find ways to maintain a presence at lower cost so a foundation exists for an easier ramp-up when times change, but again, this involves information and obtaining such information often involves a cost.

Anatomy of an Ideal Market Exit

Under ideal circumstances, the company would be gathering information on an ongoing basis about all its markets to use as a barometer and to determine how addressable or otherwise problems are which arise. In many companies, of course, such work is done on a more ad hoc basis and only when a crisis occurs do people start to gather in-depth information. In an ideal world, therefore, companies would be tapping multiple sources of information from a variety of perspectives along with making regular study of the historical cyclicity of a specific market, so as to determine how short-term or long-term the problems are. Part of the mix of information would be detailed profiles of all the competitors in each and every market along with suppliers, government entities and the legislative environment, political stability and other relevant factors. Such information, once well organized, becomes a better tool for seeing when conditions are such that a market exit is unavoidable as opposed to when things can just be ridden out until the market improves.

This was the conclusion reached by the real estate arm of Federal Industries. The port terminal operated by this division in Thunder Bay had primarily been used to move coal and, occasionally, other commodities, via the Great Lakes and St. Lawrence Seaway. But shipment tonnages had been dropping for the traditional coal product. What the company wanted to know was: Why was this happening? And what other cargo might be available?

Extensive research was conducted and showed that one of the reasons coal shipments had dropped is that western coal producers were actually finding it less costly to ship by ocean, down the Pacific coast of North America, through the Panama Canal and then to markets in Europe. There had also been some realignment of shipping along north–south routes as opposed to west–east. When it came to other commodities, such as potash, either established shipment practices were perfectly satisfactory to producers or, again, shipping routes either went east–west or north–south.

This suggested the market had changed significantly enough that an exit was probably the best strategy rather than trying to salvage the situation. But, as a business decision, it could be taken in the context of a full spectrum of information, nearly all of which was in the public domain.

What to Look For

The example of Schneider and the decision to exit certain of its markets, in spite of having volume accounts there, illustrates why certain information can streamline decision making and make the decision easier to make.

Rather than decide, in a vacuum, which markets the company wanted to exit (which would have been an emotional decision, fuelled by ego and the wrong questions), it decided to evaluate all markets on a common grid or framework. Such frameworks included information about consumers and neighborhoods, information the company had not previously assembled. This gave both a broader and deeper understanding of the markets as stand-alone entities and allowed the company to see both parallels and dissimilarities. This data was then matched to its own marketing and positioning plan before the actual markets slated for exit were picked.

Similar research preceded the decision, a few years go, for Procter & Gamble to exit the cookie business in certain of its markets. The company really had only one line or product in its cookie division; most of the competing companies had multiple lines and products. Furthermore, research showed that these companies had already achieved a certain scale in their manufacturing activities which Procter & Gamble would have to invest quite heavily to match. The competitors also had more going on in the area of new product development.

Reviewing this information — notably scale of operations and costs — led Procter & Gamble to rationalize this part of its business and concentrate on areas where the company already enjoyed a strong position. However, many companies which need to take such steps don't, because they are not willing to invest in the information which tells them they are not the low cost producer or which would reveal some other indicator pointing to an exit decision.

Where the Information Came From

Much of the information to support J. M. Schneider's eventual decision came from readily available sources. One of the main sources — and this was a case where secondary sources on their own were useful — were packages put together by the economic development offices in each of the target cities along with packages of demographic data put together by radio, television and newspapers in each of the markets. Although this data was mainly intended for prospective advertisers, it could be readily adapted to the secondary purpose of market analysis. Other public domain data tapped included city and lifestyle magazines, which revealed the flavor of various neighborhoods, plus material prepared by tourist groups. None of it was difficult to obtain and all that was really needed was the input of time to analyze and organize. But the company's decision was made much more sound because it invested the time and money, rather than Flying by the Seat of the Pants.

In the case of Federal Industries, there was an abundance of information once the researchers began looking. Maps showing coal mines, steel mills — one of the principal markets — and shipping routes, were readily available from government sources. Statistics about commodities, tonnages produced and sources of product came from the same sources. Industry associations delivered armfuls of data. Managers of port terminals and the St. Lawrence Seaway Authority were other rich sources. In short, a mix of secondary and primary sources of data once tapped, produced a wealth of information on which to base further decision making.

What is the Payoff from Better Market Exit Decisions?

One of the longer term payoffs from better market exit decisions is that the company which invests in researching such exits is less likely to exit a market and regret it later. Making market exits and then entries on a yo-yo basis racks up costs; it is very common in the retail merchandise and retail food industries for companies to do this. Department stores which give up the anchor position at a mall during a recession often want back in when the economy picks up. Some even do manage to muscle their way back in, displacing other stores which have hung in through the bad times. But the cost to the retailer which exits and then enters markets in this way, such as lease break and severance pay costs, not to mention costs incurred by the landlord, represents a rather steep price. A better stratagem may be to find ways to stick it out until the economy picks up.

For other companies, the short-term savings of a quick, unresearched market exit pale against the cost of re-entering a market where consumers may have forgotten your product, distribution channels may eye you with skepticism, and potential — former — employees may not trust you. ("Them again? How long for this time?")

Better exit decisions are, by definition, permanent and represent decisions which the company will not live to regret.

Who Benefits?

Any number of constituents benefit from an exit decision which is well-informed. Customers benefit in that, if the reasons for the market exit are shown to be short-term and the company decides to stay put, they do not suffer the loss of a chosen supplier. If, on the other hand, there are good reasons to exit, then at least everyone knows where they stand. Customers can line up other sources of supply.

A company's distribution channels also benefit if an exit decision is well-informed. Such channels will not lose a supplier or a source if the company decides to stay; if it decides to leave, then such channels can line up other items to represent.

Employees at the exiting company benefit from better exit decisions. If information shows the exit decision would be ill-advised, then they may end up keeping their jobs. If the exit goes ahead, while they may have to seek other employment, they will at least know the decision was not based on a whim but had some substance to it.

Checklist	5.4

Questions about market exits

- Why are we in this market?
- What were the original reasons to enter the market?
- What has happened to change the importance of this market?
- What are the economic, demographic, and other trends in this market?
- How have other companies in our industry fared in this market?
- Are they also exiting this market?
- Are there factors suggesting a market exit is permanent or only temporary?
- Are these factors external to our company or are they internal?
- If internal factors, can we rectify them? How will the market exit look then?
- If the factors suggesting a market exit are temporary, what is the time-frame or horizon to their removal or disappearance?
- If we go ahead and exit the market, how easy or difficult will it be to re-enter?
- Are there other ways we can maintain a presence in this market until times change?
- If we exit the market, will our competitors end up filling the vacuum and using this as leverage to gain greater share elsewhere?
- If we exit this market, what will this do to customer loyalty and customer confidence?
- How will any employees we lay off view our company? How will this affect us if we want to re-enter at a later date?
- What will be the impact on our suppliers?

Me-Too Buying Sprees: What Do We Really Need?

One of the decision-making traps into which business people too often fall centers on the "shiny new toys" that proliferate. It is particularly common, when it comes to new equipment purchases or equivalent, that decision-making of the "if it works for them, it'll work for us" variety takes over, along with a sprinkling of Old Demon Ego. This type of decision making can also extend on up the line to the decision to buy a building, even if it means having one built from scratch.

How Purchase Decisions Happen

Under ideal circumstances purchasing decisions are made by a company's procurement specialists who make detailed study and weigh all the options available before making a commitment to purchase something. In many cases, procurement requirements are put out to tender and suppliers have to submit bids to be considered as suppliers. The image created is one of orderly, rational decision making based on a corpus of information. To be fair to people in procurement, many purchasing departments are run this way.

But that not all purchase decisions are made this way will not surprise anyone familiar with business. Sometimes, even in situations where bids have been asked for, the requirement to go with the lowest bidder does not necessarily lead to the best purchase decision. Then, there are cases where someone "upstairs" decides that the company has to Keep Up With the Jones's and so an order is issued to purchase something. Competitor A purchased new production equipment? We have to have it too! Competitor B has a new LAN (local area network)? We have to have one too! There's a real fear, nowadays, particularly with technology, of being seen to be old-fashioned or behind the times, which can have a huge impact on how corporations set their priorities.

Sometimes, there's a good reason to be a copycat. If the new equipment will halve a competitor's production costs relative to yours, they will also have the latitude to lower prices. Not matching them, in some way, (although this doesn't necessarily mean purchasing the exact same item), may put your company at a serious disadvantage. The new LAN may enable them to do more with fewer people, lowering their head count and therefore their payroll. Your company may again be at a serious disadvantage. But you won't know if this is the case, if you don't first ask the right questions and get the right answers.

Then, as the case of the newsprint maker showed, out-and-out copying can be fiscally hazardous. Plunging ahead with me-too purchasing, the company later came to regret such blind imitation.

What Gets Forgotten

An obvious first question, when Competitor A buys the new equipment, is: Why did they purchase it? And why now? It may be the case that the purchase was one long-planned to replace machinery fast becoming obsolete. It may be that the cost of ongoing maintenance had become so astronomical that new equipment was the only viable option. And it may also be the case that the cost of purchasing the equipment and the way it had to be financed will push any thought of cost savings and subsequent price reductions off to a distant horizon. Finding out the answers to such simple questions may actually indicate a better decision, for your company, is to wait to buy new equipment, until the next generation of machinery is available and you have enough cash to finance it easily. Making the decision without the facts, on an information-less basis, will not lead to this wisdom.

Another question or group of questions which is rarely asked is: What are the objectives for the purchase? Can they be met in other ways? What will the purchase improve? What will not be improved? The stampede to purchase Windows '95 when it first appeared (or its subsequent upgrades) illustrates the fallacy of me-too purchasing. Many companies, having once installed this software for fear of being seen to be behind-the-times without it, have capability that is not being used and is not needed, meaning it will never be used at their companies, while their hard drive space is seriously over-consumed by the program. The fact this software often takes longer to boot up than earlier versions is another issue the me-too crowd overlooked.

The wisdom of asking a few hard questions about a purchase decision, especially for a major purchase, is illustrated by the case of a petroleum refining company which was in the process of considering upgrading its yield accounting software. This was not the purchase of some off-the-shelf software in a box for a few hundred dollars but a $1 million plus purchase of manufacturing software. What had been the benefits in other process industries from purchasing this software? the company wondered. Had they been able to reduce the number of reports or the headcount in their yield accounting areas? What were some of the benefits of this software? Was it really state-of-the-art or were only a few companies using it? This last question was important, for the company considered that anything less than state-of-the-art would likely lead to hiring problems if there were not sufficient numbers of people trained in this software available in the labor market.

Since the answers to their questions were not recorded anywhere, they had to commission independent research to check out the issues. This revealed that only certain industries were using this software for process operations; in this particular refiner's jurisdiction, processors of distilled products and brewed products still had to do certain yield accounting procedures by hand, to comply with laws that were somewhat antiquated. Other refiners were indeed using the software but had only noticed minimal reductions in numbers of reports and in their headcount for this function. Other information was obtained to answer the other questions; in the end, the refiner did decide to purchase the software but was well aware of what the cost-benefits would be and could present the decision to management in this light.

When it comes to even more significant purchases, such as erecting a building from scratch, even a casual observer of business would likely think such decisions should be subjected to even more pre-purchase scrutiny than a mere piece of software.

In theory, long before any decision is made to purchase land or go into the ground, anyone inclined to build, including property developers, would carefully study the market and the future needs of businesses, including a study of growth rates and the types of buildings along with the sizes of spaces that will be needed. Some consideration of how buildings can be built so as to be adaptable to future needs, given the rapid rate of change in society, would also enter the picture.

In reality, the evidence suggests that few, if any, decisions to put up office and factory space are made in this way. Instead, they tend also to be made in a spirit of Keeping up with the Jones's. The frenzy of office building in the late 1980s in many large North American cities, suggests that property developers were basing their decisions on anything but the facts. Sleek new office towers rose skyward from business cores. Cranes towered everywhere the eye could see. Rents rose to astronomical levels. Then the bubble burst.

To understand what went wrong, one only needs look at why this situation developed in the first place. And the reason is that developers didn't bother to look at the right information. What all of them should have asked is: What is the real rate of business growth? How many of the companies occupying less than 3,000 square feet now are going to grow to a size where they will require a full floor or more of space (usually at least 10,000 square feet)? What are the business growth rate projections over the next 25 years?

Had they bothered to ask such questions, few developers would have indulged in a buying spree on new buildings. Basic statistical data, available from most governments, will show you that business creation rates just about even out with business dissolution rates in any given year, meaning there is little net new business creation per annum. Statistics, widely available, show that most businesses — upwards of 70–75% in North America — employ five or fewer people and that this has been a constant for years. And, had the developers bothered to look at statistical projections, they would have noticed that, once the Baby Boomers start retiring in the year 2010, there will be fewer and fewer businesses around, meaning there will be fewer prospective tenants.

The same lack of informed decision making can also sabotage companies which decide they must have a new factory. One of the questions which very rarely gets asked is: What can be done to retrofit our existing space? What can be done to change our modus operandi to use what we already have? And, if these questions show that nothing can be done, a further question is: What other existing spaces can be transformed to meet our needs? It is generally true that at any given time, while new buildings arise on land that has been assembled specifically for that purpose, not far away large empty buildings lie unused, simply because a tenant or owner cannot be found for them. This tends to be more of a problem in North America where the abundance of land in wide open spaces leads to this kind of uneconomical practice, although recent press reports suggest that, as of the late 1990s, Asian cities were feeling the pinch too, as over-ambitious building had led to a glut of space.

Anatomy of an Ideal Purchasing Decision

The example of the refiner and their willingness to invest a minimal amount of money — at the time, around $3,000 — for a major purchase decision indicates how, in an ideal world, all purchase decisions would be made, especially when significant capital outlays are involved. Making an ideal, well-informed purchase decision involves going beyond information supplied by the actual suppliers or sellers of the item to a broader environment. In cases where others have gone before and made purchases, tapping their knowledge becomes indispensable. In the case of purchases which might be termed mission-critical, in addition to learning about other companies' experiences with the item, there's an opportunity to find out about other products or services which are in development and could emerge within the time horizon expected for the use of the purchase. There is no point in purchasing a piece of equipment with an expected life span of ten years if, within the next three, something vastly superior will be available. In such cases, information obtained prior to making the purchase decision can re-orient priorities, such as to making use of what is already installed and perhaps investing in maintaining that for just a little bit longer.

Knowing about the external environment can also assist with other types of major commitment, such as a lease for space. A testing organization, specializing in textile testing, was debating whether to renew the lease on one of its sites in the New York City area. Business had dropped but the testing company wasn't sure if this was due to market conditions or some other factor.

Independent research to investigate a range of issues from different constituents was commissioned; customers, suppliers, competitors, market and industry watchers were all tapped. Those involved were from all stages of the textile chain: from fiber and yarn manufacturers down to dry cleaners. The research showed shifts in the marketplace and changes in demand that the testing organization had perhaps not kept as up-to-date as it might have. As a result, they came to the conclusion they had less of a market problem and more of a marketing problem. Further decision-making about the lease on the lab proceeded on an informed basis.

What to Look For

The size and significance of the purchase to be made will have the greatest bearing on what to look for in the way of information. So will the role of the purchase at the organization — does it have a "make or break" impact? — along with its expected shelf life. In the case of the refiner in the market for software, the decision makers knew that, once purchased, the budget would not be available to correct any mistakes. While the seller of the software — the package chosen was MRP II — would undoubtedly back their product, there was still an element of "All Sales Final" which is often the case with business purchases. Once the building has been put up, a company can't turn round and say: "We don't like it. Take it down and start over."

In the case of the newsprint company, it forgot to look closely at how well-informed its competitors were — or weren't, as the case was. Since other newsprint makers were also oblivious to the trend in recycling, everyone blundered together. This suggests that, should any company so desire, careful use of disinformation about its plans could lure a foolhardy competitor into financial difficulties; as discussed earlier in this book, information found in sources such as the Web, always need to be checked out, for this reason.

Where the Information Came From

Every so often, there will be articles conveniently published that describe a company's experience with a product or service, such as MRP II, but when there are not — or are very few, as was the case for the petroleum refiner — more creative methods have to be used. Product literature was obtained about the software, the few available articles were retrieved but the real "meat" of the information came from the process industries themselves. Key managers at twenty companies in different industries, including other refiners, were tapped for their experiences. From these interviews, several essential facts emerged, to provide a blueprint for further decision making.

In the case of the textile testing lab, information came from a range of sources, including published data along with primary research interviews with industry experts. The secondary source material supplied the foundation and the leads to further research; the interviews with these leads provided the answers. As with so many research undertakings, there was a cumulative effect from tapping a sequence of sources but none was particularly difficult to access. As this book has repeatedly emphasized: *the information to make better, more informed decisions is readily available.*

As for the developers on their me-too buying spree, all the data to paint a realistic picture of the future came from readily available government sources, information which they, as tax payers, had already paid to have created.

What is the Payoff from Better Buying Decisions?

Making a better buying decision might sometimes mean deferring a purchase, or sometimes spending more than originally intended. The payoff is therefore not measured so much in terms of dollars but in terms of reduced risk. Just imagine, when buying a re-sale home, what a purchaser might learn if they could speak to all the people who had lived in the house since it was built? Explanations of the house's quirks and tips on how to deal with problems would pour from the lips of previous occupants. Even if some of the information wasn't positive, the buyer could decide to go ahead (or not) with their eyes fully opened.

This is the payoff when business purchases are based on a solid foundation of information. The risks are known or at least unearthed and the company can go into the situation with eyes open.

The dollar impact may not really come until later when lower maintenance costs or lower recruitment costs or some similar tangible benefit becomes evident.

Who Benefits?

Employees and managers at a company benefit the most from more informed purchase decisions, either in terms of how they end up being asked to perform their work or in long-term job continuity. A company which puts up a new building and then finds itself with serious cash flow problems likely won't be one handing out raises or sending people on training courses; they are more likely to be countenancing layoffs. Like so many bad decisions, bad buying practices have both an immediate and longer term ripple effect on the company.

Checklist   5.5

Questions about purchases

- Do we really need this?
- What could we retrofit or make "adaptive re-use" of instead of this purchase?
- Why are we looking at this purchase?
- If it is because our competitors have made such purchases, why did they buy?
- Have they been satisfied with their purchase? What did they gain?
- What will be the competitive or marketplace repercussions if we don't buy?
- If our competitors have bought, why did they do so now, as opposed to a year ago or a year from now?

- If non-competitor companies have bought, what has been their experience?
- What benefits have they derived?
- What are some of the negatives?
- How are we going to pay for this?
- If it has to be financed, can we afford the financing?
- If we finance this, will we still have enough latitude to finance other items, to address needs we don't yet know about?
- Will purchasing this item reduce or raise our costs?
- How will the purchase affect our headcount?
- Will the purchase have a positive or negative impact on our training costs?
- Will it enable us to lower our prices or will we have to raise them?
- Is our projected growth rate or the future demand for what we do indicating that we should make this purchase?

Who Should We Sell To? And What Can We Do About "The Ones That Got Away"?

Although it might be difficult to decide about market exits or acquisitions, many people would assume that decisions about customers — or clients — are never difficult. Knowing who a company sells to, whom it should sell to and all the permutations in between are surely at the "no-brainer" end of the scale.

Sadly, this is often not the case, as many large companies are often surprisingly weak in the area of customer service and customer retention; their continued existence owes itself to momentum and money built up at a time when markets were less competitive.

How Customer Decisions Happen

There are three broad categories of customers: current customers, prospective customers, lost accounts. For most companies the objectives should be fairly clear; retain the existing customers, win back the lost accounts and land new business. Around these three categories swirl a number of customer-related decisions: pricing, after-sales service, communications, product development and more; in theory, all companies are well set up to handle their customers and the decisions which arise. The customer base is well-known and well segmented. A number of marketing strategies have been devised to reach these segments, such strategies being well executed in the field by a top notch sales force. Any customer feedback or complaints are swiftly handled by a crack customer service team. A well-oiled machine not only retains these customers but regularly lands new ones.

In reality, any number of companies have "chinks in their armor" over customer issues and related decisions. Some large companies, in spite of state-of-the art technology, do not know who all their customers are. If the company has multiple locations or divisions, it is not even known when there are multiple contact points and multiple sales to these large customers. Any customer lists are often in need of updating. It is not uncommon for a company to have a customer list with defunct companies or deceased individuals listed as "customers." Given this level of disorganization, is it any wonder that decisions about customers are often made in a vacuum?

A loss of common sense can also prove a company's undoing with its customers, as almost happened to the waste management company. Besotted with the idea of market segmentation, this organization lost sight of the fact that customers, in its business, do not really distinguish much between waste haulers, since the purchase decision usually turns on price. This is why route density is usually the best way to profitability. By imagining customers could be determined by segmentation in its particular line of work, the company was losing its grip on reality.

The same would have been true for a courier firm which decided its market segment was law firms or stock brokers. Fine, if all such firms are located in a narrow radius from one another but not if they are flung out over a 240-square-mile territory. Thinking such a company does have a segmentable market begs the question; even if it does sign up 75% of the law firms in a city, the fact they are located closely together — route density — takes precedence over the type of industry they are in.

What Gets Forgotten

What companies also tend to forget is that their customers inhabit a world of change every bit as much as they do. Signing up the account is not enough; it is necessary to stay up-to-date about it. This was discovered by a natural gas company which wanted to learn more about its volume accounts. Prior to any research being started, the gas company opined that most of its large volume customers were likely in the automotive or construction sectors. Since these sectors are particularly vulnerable to downturns in the economy, the company wanted to know how vulnerable it was, by association, to the next recession.

Although this utility knew who its volume accounts were, it soon became apparent that no attempts had been made to keep informed about just what these accounts were doing. Rather than serving the automotive or construction sectors, the utility was actually heavily exposed to the consumer goods sector, with business services a close second. This meant the gas company was indeed exposed to the next downturn but from completely different directions then the ones it imagined.

What the utility had forgotten — or overlooked — are some of the broader trends in the marketplace, the trend away from so-called "sunset" industries, such as automotive and construction, to the "sunrise" industries, computer-based technologies, electronics, which had transformed its customer base. If the utility had not discovered this transformation, many decisions about programs, pricing and packaging could have turned out to be ill-advised and a means to driving the customers away.

On the opposite side of the coin, what can equally be forgotten, in this case by the customers, is who you are. A vinyl siding manufacturer set out to test awareness among its distributors, otherwise known as trade accounts. Given that vinyl siding is close to being a commodity, this issue of awareness was key to future profitability. What the manufacturer discovered is that many distributors confused their suppliers, ran the names together or didn't know them in the first place. Name recognition was very weak. This suggested that some of the company's planned expenditures on advertising needed to be re-thought and an incentive program needed to be redesigned. In short, a number of decisions the siding manufacturer had been about to make had to be re-formulated in the light of available information. But had such decision not been reformulated, several thousands of dollars would have been wasted on the wrong initiatives.

For a midwest ink manufacturer, both sets of circumstances converged to show how out of touch with some of its customers it was. Concerned about the impact of discontinuing one of its brand names, the company had an external survey conducted. Once the customer list was made available from the corporate office — which seemed reluctant to share within the organization, a not-infrequent situation — not only were one third of the "customers" found to be anything but, most didn't recognize the brand name of the ink they were regularly purchasing! Information was definitely lacking on all sides!

Anatomy of an Ideal Customer Decision

The first attribute of any ideal decision made around customers is: make no assumptions. The second attribute is: gather information — a lot of it! Many companies actually scrimp on customer surveys or avoid them altogether. Few ever invest in lost account research to find out what went wrong.

Were they to do so, they would quickly realize the benefits, provided the right questions were asked. How significant are we to your company? they would ask customers. If the answer comes back negative the next question is: Why not? What do we have to do to change this? Prime Computer, by asking the right questions before contract cancellations started pouring in — which is when many companies would finally take action — was enabled, by the information obtained, to take corrective action to retain its accounts.

While direct contact with the customers would seem like the most obvious way to gather information about customers, there are many other sources. Customer companies may well be profiled in articles in trade magazines. They may publish annual reports, if they are publicly traded. They may produce catalogs, newsletters or other publications, their people may speak at conferences. They may exhibit at trade shows. There is an almost never-ending supply of information to tap about customers; who they are, what they do, who their customers are. Any decisions which have to be made about a company's customer base should therefore be made in an information-rich environment.

Keeping information up-to-date is equally important for any lost accounts a company might want to win back. Information from a variety of sources can be used for leverage for this purpose, as was discovered by a trust company. Stung by customer defections from some very prestigious pension plan sponsors, the trust company wanted to learn what it had done wrong and how it might make amends.

Interviews were therefore conducted with key decision makers at the plan sponsors which quickly revealed the defections were attributable to two causes: mistakes by the trust company and appointments made at the board level. While the board appointments were less within the trust company's control, it at least had the satisfaction of knowing it was not to blame in such cases. For the other accounts, enough information was obtained to use as a basis for winning back the account.

Finding out what your customers — or prospective customers — really want is another key foundation to better decision-making. The insurance specialist mentioned in Chapter 3 did not want to hear what the marketplace wanted and so lost an opportunity. This was not the case for Norstan, a telecom industry supplier, which set out to learn not only who its customers were but what they needed in the way of long-distance services.

While the company had set out on the exercise with certain assumptions — about the network services the company offered and how to price those offerings — the messages which came back from the customers suggested unmet needs in the area of voice, data and video convergence, which in turn suggested additional business opportunities to the company. By gathering detailed information from a range of accounts, Norstan had a better blueprint for further customer service and its own decision making. Some companies don't ever bother to ask what their customers want!

What to Look For

Having some sense of what an ideal or desirable customer looks like is often the first step to better customer decisions. A mid-west bank, noted for asset-based lending, had noticed a decline in demand for its services at a time when the economy was improving, since cash was readily available and the cost of regular financing low. It therefore set out to identify prospective customers. Rather than a "shot-in-the-dark" exercise, the bank knew enough about its ideal customer to shape the search productively.

What is perhaps more surprising to those unfamiliar with information resources is just how much data there was in the public domain to answer questions such as: who already does asset-based borrowing? What is their current financial picture? Who are their current lenders? How much financing might they need? Making decisions about which of these companies to target could then proceed in a cost-effective way.

Where the Information Comes From

Even when companies do have information about their customers available, they often overlook the resources at their fingertips and how to exploit them. The customer's financial well-being is one aspect but equally important is information about the customer's expansion plans, planned relocations, new product introductions, profit plans and cost-cutting measures, human resources goals and the like.

Such information can provide a detailed framework for the supplier company's new product development, business growth strategies and more.

In the case of the gas utility interested in knowing more about its volume accounts, most of the information came from materials produced by the volume accounts themselves: their annual reports, catalogs, press releases and newsletters. Articles produced by third parties filled in any gaps while all the information was verified by phone with the target companies.

A mix of secondary and primary sources provided the information needed by the Midwest asset-based lender. For publicly traded companies, SEC filings were first tapped and then refined via phone interviews with Controllers, VPs of Finance, or Treasurers. For privately held companies, a mix of credit reports, UCC filings and article information was rounded out by interviews with similar financial people. Time-consuming? Yes, but all relatively easily available information.

In contrast, the customer awareness information sought by the vinyl siding manufacturer had to come straight from the distributors themselves; only the managers or sales people could give the insight and reveal their awareness of competing product or describe brand recognition. Such information is rarely available from other sources.

The same was true for the trust company; only the plan sponsors themselves could provide the answers. But most did willingly, indicating once again, that key decision making information is readily available to anyone who wants to take the time and trouble to tap it. For a company like Norstan, the information also had to come directly from customers, meaning only primary research was conducted. This was also a case when turning to an outside party improved the process; customers often don't reveal everything if you approach them directly but will happily chat, at length, with a third party over the neutral and somewhat anonymous medium of the telephone.

What is the Payoff from Better Customer Decisions?

One of the more obvious payoffs from better informed customer decisions is better customer retention. The much higher cost of winning a new account versus retaining an existing account is now well-known and undisputed. Any company which can retain its customer base while adding new customers is much better positioned for long term growth and greater profitability.

In the case of Prime Computer, retaining just 25% of its customer base conserved several million dollars in revenue while for the trust company, winning back any of its plan sponsors, which had multimillion dollar assets under management, bought fee revenue of a million or more dollars for each account.

Who Benefits?

Better customer decisions not only benefit the supplier company but also the customers themselves. Knowing more about the customers and their needs increases the likelihood of meeting those needs; products that the customers especially like won't be withdrawn, angering the customers. Greater customer retention means greater profitability, meaning shareholders of the company benefit; if dollars are being spent, via sales efforts, to land additional accounts, rather than win replacement business, the sales force benefits and will also be more highly motivated. This means all the other employees in the company indirectly benefit.

Checklist   5.6

Questions about current customers

- Who are our customers?
- Do the companies we *think* are our customers still buy from us?
- If not, are they still in business? If so, who do they buy from?
- Who are our customers' customers?
- How are our customers' businesses changing?
- How many divisions of each customer buys from us?
- How many of our divisions do business with each customer?
- Are we considered a major or minor supplier by each customer?
- Which of our competitors sells to each customer?
- What else could we be selling to each of our customers?

Questions about former customers

- Are they still in business?
- If so, what does their business look like now? How has it changed since we last did business with them?
- Why did they stop buying from us?
- Who are they buying from today?
- What current needs do they have?
- What aspects of our company have changed since we last did business with them?
- Where are the points of leverage for rebuilding the business?
- Who can we or should we approach?

Questions about prospective customers

- Are they currently purchasing our type of product or service?
- Who do they currently buy from?
- How do we compare to their current supplier?
- Who are *their* customers?
- What changes going on in their business or industry can we address?
- Who should we contact?
- What procedures do they follow for purchasing?
- How many decision makers or buying influences are there for what we sell?

Diversify or Die? Or is There a Third Option?

There is no single reason why companies decide to diversify away from their main line of business but one of the reasons is market saturation; when markets start to offer less potential for future growth, companies start looking elsewhere for sources of new business. The same is true when markets mature or products mature; many businesses then find themselves needing to make long-term strategic choices about where future business will come from. And this often means getting into a completely different line of endeavor. Another driver of diversification may be a sizeable pool of cash from which the company wishes to realize better returns and to gain more value for shareholders.

How Diversification Decisions Happen

In theory, a decision to diversify is based on a careful and deliberate process when a company recognizes that growth in its existing markets is slowing and product life cycles are coming to an end. This recognition of the need to add new revenue streams to the business is part of a careful and well thought out procedure for identifying opportunities for future profits. In companies where diversification is a deliberate and careful strategy, consideration is first given to finding new markets for existing product lines before what are known as green field operations are considered. Such companies also look carefully at diversification opportunities where the expertises of current executives have a natural fit; industries in which the company has no exposure whatsoever and therefore no knowledge are not really actively considered.

In reality, diversification often happens when executives get itchy feet, such as the case of the railcar manufacturer which diversified into eyecare services. Often, the amount of money available to diversify goes to the head of whoever is in charge of the decision; there's enough of a cushion available so that, even if they make a mistake, the parent company can absorb the blow. Many diversification initiatives are a clear case of Old Demon Ego decision making.

And in situations where Old Demon Ego isn't running the show, companies are sometimes under time pressures to make a choice about diversification but not the wisest choice, meaning Fly-by-the-Seat-of-Your-Pants decisions get made. This could well have been the fate of the grain products company which was considering diversification into shrimp aquaculture as discussed earlier in this book. While it is true that breads and biscuits are food products much the way shrimps are, the processes to produce each item and the type of business each entails are wildly different. Although in this case the executives at the current company were wise enough, once they had all the information in hand, to recognize that shrimp aquaculture was a high-risk diversification opportunity, they were at least able to assess the situation before going ahead. Many companies would not have taken this route and would not have invested in information before plunging ahead. Or, what many companies would have done is look at the increasing demand for seafood, notably in the retail food service sector of the economy, and figure that shrimp aquaculture must be a no-brainer given this huge demand.

What Gets Forgotten

What people fail to realize, when they seek to diversify away from their known line of business, is that every industry or business looks simple enough to run from the outside looking in. Usually, when you are inside looking out, it is a different situation entirely; while it is true that there are commonalities to all businesses in how they are run — accounting, tax filing, adhering to employment law in hiring practices, giving good service to customers, etc. — most businesses do have some element or core to them that operators must know. This core expertise might have something to do with how to make the product, how to distribute the product, how to present it to customers, how to control costs, or a combination of such factors; rarely is it knowledge that one could gain in textbook fashion.

Most failed diversifications can be attributed to overlooking these special success factors or expertises. It is also true that many diversifications don't work out because people do not look closely enough at what the long term profitability and potential is in the industry they are entering. If profit margins are shrinking in the current line of business, it will not help overall revenues if the company diversifies into another industry where profit margins are also similarly eroding. This becomes a case of going "out of the frying pan into the fire." Yet the information to answer these questions can be readily obtained.

But once the glamor of diversification has smitten the executives at a company, very rarely does one of them say to the others: What could we do with our existing products or services in terms of line extensions or added value as a way of growing our business? Have these options been fully explored?

Even when the line of business chosen for diversification *is* close to the company's current activities, more information can help shape the venture into a successful one. A few years ago, Commonwealth Hospitality, as an operator of hotels, was looking around for other niches or markets where the company could diversify while building on existing expertises.

The business development staff knew that there were a number of distressed hotel properties around as the recession took its toll. The company also knew the banks holding mortgages and loans on these properties needed outside expertise to help run them, but how could Commonwealth tap into the opportunity?

Just plunging ahead and hoping to make connections didn't seem like a very smart strategy, so the company commissioned research to learn more about the mechanics of the interim hotel management business. The information which this process provided gave a blueprint for further action. The appropriate contacts for networking with, on the bank side, turned out to be in the "special loans" department, the euphemism most banks used for really troubled lending situations. But it was only after a certain amount of digging that the existence of such departments would be acknowledged by financial institutions. Perhaps more surprising was the nature of the competition. Commonwealth Hospitality had expected other hotel companies to be the competition; instead, smaller, highly specialized firms, often run by entrepreneurs, made up the bulk of the competitors.

Anatomy of an Ideal Diversification

In an ideal diversification strategy, long before a company actually needed to make such moves, information would be gathered and analyzed to create a repository and tracking system of opportunities that might be out there. Certainly, in an ideal situation, companies would avoid those "do or die" situations where diversification has to happen on a panic-stricken basis. They would instead explore multiple opportunities and look more closely at the fit with existing businesses. They would also have a better understanding of the costs of starting up in a totally different industry or what would be involved to integrate an existing business if they made an acquisition as their way of diversifying away from existing businesses.

Just as the rule of thumb with expansion is to expand close to home geographically, the rule of thumb with successful diversifications is to diversify fairly close to your existing business. An analysis of all diversifications undertaken by businesses throughout recorded history is beyond the scope of this book but should a student of business take a look at diversifications, those which were successful will show that the companies hewed fairly closely to this line. The case cited earlier of the railcar manufacturer which branched out into eyecare is a classic example of a company wandering too far from its roots to redirect its business. A better diversification strategy would have been to look at businesses which meshed more closely with the existing activity. Railroad track and ties, railroad maintenance equipment, value-added containers for rail shipment or another transportation modality, such as shipping, would all have been better ideas.

What to Look For

What many companies fail to look at when they diversify, in contrast to when they make an acquisition, is the real cost of entering a completely different industry. Other issues which get overlooked include the level of competition in this sector; failure to undertake a full competitive analysis of an industry you are entering — which is often a reflection of the unwillingness to invest the money in such an investigation — will frequently undo the novice once they get themselves set up. It is also equally important with a diversification to look at how stable the customer base is and what potential is offered for future growth. Another key issue to examine is how cyclical the new industry is and, if it is cyclical, does it run in synch with the current business or is it counter-cyclical to the current business; if one of the objectives of diversification is to improve the revenue stream, balancing out cyclicity surely must be one of the top objectives.

These and other key questions should have been asked by the auto parts manufacturer looking to diversify into tennis racquets and tennis wear. In spite of the practice of auto manufacturers to buy on contract and commit a fair way down the road, automobiles are still a cyclical industry, dependent on consumer spending. But then, so is tennis dependent on consumer spending. And items like tennis racquets and tennis wear fall much more squarely into the category of discretionary spending than even automobiles do.

Where the Information Came From

As with all business decisions, the information to make a wise diversification choice does not come from any one place or one source. In the case of the shrimp aquaculture business which the milled products company investigated, only a certain amount of basic or foundation data came from print publications or databases. And most of the information which was available in these sources was of a technical nature, covering issues such as water temperature and level of salinity for a successful shrimp farm, not discussions of marketing factors. These sources, however, did provide a useful starting point and allowed those doing the research to identify government sources, notably experts on staff in the U.S. government, who were extremely well-informed about shrimp aquaculture operations. These people were able to provide a considerable number of do's and don'ts, information which was confirmed and elaborated on by those who were currently operating shrimp aquaculture farms.

But perhaps the best information of all came from those who were failed operators; the exit rate or failure rate from shrimp farming is quite high and the stories such failed operators were willing to share indicated how high-risk this whole area of endeavor is. Given that losses can quickly climb in the first year or two of operation to around the $12 million mark, this information was critical. The most valuable piece of information which came out of the whole information gathering exercise was the fact that the wind and land factors were equally as important as the sea factors in successful shrimp farming. On this basis, the food manufacturer considering this diversification was able to drop two sites from its short list under consideration. Had this information not been obtained, the company may have gone ahead with those sites and would have incurred considerable losses as a result.

In the case of Commonwealth Hospitality, little information came from secondary sources; interim hotel management is one example of the type of topic which comes up in business information gathering fairly often: a highly focussed and specialized area of endeavor which does not lend itself to a lot of discussion or coverage in the press. Statistically, it's the type of "industry" — if it can even be called that — which ends up in the NEC classification in government reports; even those involved in interim hotel management, such as the banks, do not wish to publicize their participation. Most of the information therefore came from tracking down bankers, hotel managers and hotel owners and interviewing them about how distressed hotel properties were handled.

What is the Payoff from Better Diversification Decisions?

Much like the market entries discussed earlier, diversification tends to be a higher profile activity than some other initiatives companies undertake; while the plan to diversify can be kept quiet, once a company starts buying land, putting up buildings or purchasing advertising space far from home, others can quickly see what you're up to.

Better diversification decisions therefore mean a company can avoid the twin perils of financial losses on a bad move as well as loss of face in the public eye. Picking the right diversification opportunity means more prestige as well as profitability. Funds conserved from avoiding a bad choice can be made available for better choices at a later date.

Who Benefits?

Shareholders, if the company is publicly traded, can be among the earlier beneficiaries of better divestiture decisions. Smart moves by a company tend to boost stock prices. This, in turn, will attract more investment.

For employees at a company in the process of diversifying, there are the obvious benefits of more opportunity, perhaps postings overseas, and more promise of employment continuity. Poor diversifications tend to have a ripple effect; first the employees at the new venture lose their jobs when things don't work out, then the employees at the original entity are "downsized" as cost cutting seeps back up the chain. Management also benefits from making good diversification decisions, if only because the board or owners will have the confidence to back future endeavors — while keeping the current executives in their jobs.

Checklist   5.7

Questions prior to diversification

- Why do we need to diversify?
- Are our existing markets totally saturated?
- Are there overlooked opportunities to re-invest in existing operations?
- What could we do to increase sales to existing customers?
- If we diversify, will the "sum of the parts" be greater than the whole? Or will it drain resources?
- What expertise do we have that lends itself to businesses which might be dissimilar to ours?
- How far away from our core business can we safely venture?
- If our business is cyclical, what opportunities are there in counter-cyclical businesses which would produce a good fit?
- Can we fund any diversification from our own resources or would we need outside financing?
- Will the new business activity cannibalize sales from our existing, core business?

Questions during diversification selection

- How closely does our chosen industry or activity fit with our current line of business?
- What special expertise makes others in this industry successful?
- What factors have led others to fail or exit this line of business?
- What are the true costs of diversifying into this business?
- How many more experienced competitors will we face?
- What will their response likely be to our entering this industry?
- What are the "hidden differences" between this line of endeavor and our own?
- How will our customers view this diversification?
- Will they perceive that we're "abandoning ship" and line up alternate suppliers?

Who Do We Compete Against? How Can We Compete Against Them?

Many companies go through life quite happily paying only minimal attention to their competition. But these companies tend to be very, very small enterprises: the shoe repair guy, the dry cleaner, the convenience store. Such businesses have competition but since their custom comes from local traffic, there is a territoriality which often protects such businesses, meaning they and their competition rarely meet.

But once a business achieves a certain size or if a business is intent on growth and becoming much larger, then knowing about the competition becomes crucial to success. Although some might argue that if you concentrate on good customer service you will always be OK, in the very real, real world of business, such is idealism. Competitors may have many plans to take your customers away, in spite of how well you are serving them. Competitors may have plans to dominate the industry and enter into hostile takeovers against you. Competitors may have plans to sew up suppliers on exclusive contracts and put you at a disadvantage. They may be developing new products or services which will wipe your business off the face of earth. That's why it is absolutely essential for businesses to truly, really know their competition.

How Competitors are Selected

If competitive forces were to be studied in an ideal environment, then a company would sit down and look at the issue customer by customer and would find out who they compete against with each and every customer, on a case-by-case basis. Then, they would take this a step further and look at both market segments and geographic territories and identify the "league" they play in, as regards other companies providing similar services or products in those markets and territories. They would further recognize that competition is not the same across all markets or segments meaning that major competitors in one part of the market or country will be minor competitors somewhere else and that the picture of competition is constantly changing.

In this ideal world, companies would also look at substitutes: the alternative products, services or technologies which customers could choose in lieu of what they offer. They would also recognize that government policies, the legal environment and other factors affect the playing field and could displace their business, making these competitive forces to monitor as well.

In practice, competition is very rarely identified in such a precise manner. And a variety of decision making styles come into play. Most companies like to think they go head-to-head with the number one company in the industry, meaning that Old Demon Ego is in on the act as to how the decision is made. Another favorite pastime in selecting competition is to just choose whichever companies were competed against in the past, a demonstration of the belief that the company already has all the answers; the fact that certain companies which were competitors in the past may have gone out of business or may have exited the market doesn't enter the thinking. It is even possible to take this to a more abstract level and use an "ivory tower" approach, choosing companies which you believe ought to be competitors.

What Gets Forgotten

What most companies overlook, when they sit down to decide who their competition is, is that taking an inside-out view of the marketplace is rarely an accurate view. It is really crucial, when deciding on the field of competition, which can be a vital decision if it is to influence marketing and sales, advertising and promotion, manufacturing costs and many other aspects of the organization, that the customer's view of competition should ultimately rule decision making. Who the customers see as competition is therefore one of the elements which must be understood but rarely is, simply because this results in conclusions which are not as "pretty" as those reached in a vacuum.

It is equally important to find out who suppliers consider to be in the same league as your company; if they are providing products and services to your competitors but are cutting you out of the loop, because they don't think you "count" as much, this can put you at a disadvantage. And how about dealers and distributors? They often have a very strong handle on how companies are ranked and who truly competes against whom but their input is rarely asked for. Even associations which represent all companies in the industry have information to share on the subject; they know which companies control the agenda in the industry and which merely are affected by the agenda.

Anatomy of an Ideal Competitive Decision

In an ideal situation, a company would go literally from customer to customer, especially its major accounts, and find out in their eyes which companies are the true competitors. This would involve finding out if these companies are continual or perpetual competitors or if they only enter the situation on certain types of order. In cases where purchasing is put out to bid or tender, the company would find out how often it is on the short list for each customer and who else is on this list. Companies would also identify cases where their customer single sources and chooses only their firm.

Not finding out via real-world information about who the competitors really are can leave a company making decisions with negative consequences. Not knowing, for example, who really owns your competition can lead to erroneous assessment of a competitor's strengths and weaknesses.

This was the situation facing a company in the IVR industry, as it's known, or Interactive Voice Response. In this particular segment of IVR, which provides what are known as telepersonals or chat lines, there is a tendency by industry players to hide from public view. Most of the companies offering such services run ads in alternative weeklies or have Web sites but there is little else about them which is visible.

Upon investigation, this particular company discovered that its real competition was concentrated in the hands of a few, very large and reasonably well financed players. Had the company just relied on impressions from ads and other public manifestations from the competitors, this fact — and the true nature of competition — would never have been known.

The names listed as the operators under the ads or on Web sites were usually just the names of business units or divisions of much larger enterprises. There was nothing particularly underhand about this — many organizations have various divisions or business units for operating purposes. But not tracing these names back and finding out about true ownership would have created a mirage — and left the company in the IVR business at a disadvantage.

In an ideal situation, as mentioned above, a company would also open the agenda to finding out about substitutes. Are these substitutes as attractive to the customers? What prompts the customer to make the substitution? Such questions and others would be asked, but they would be asked as part of ongoing tracking of the competition which should be a very information-rich activity, carried out 365 days a year.

Substitute competition is really what the pharmaceutical industry, discussed earlier, faces in the form of the alternative health movement. Consumers who are deliberately avoiding chemical drug preparations are a competitive threat as much as the alternative therapies being offered, and they need to be seen as such. Even the increasing incidence of adverse drug reactions or antibiotic-resistant strains of bacteria are forms of competition which need to be analyzed to find ways to compete against them.

Likewise, the newsprint manufacturers discussed in another chapter of this book need to see alternative media — such as CD–ROMS — as competition; illiteracy levels also need to be viewed in the same light. (But most newsprint makers, when asked would likely cite other newsprint manufacturers as their competition — and would stop there. Something of an "ivory-tower" approach to identifying whom you compete against....)

Such substitute competition (or displacement competition) should figure in the competitive agenda of the tobacco companies discussed earlier — the alternative uses for the tobacco plant, the increase in non-nicotine-based treatments and therapies — but most do not pay attention to these competitive forces. This means they miss an opportunity to tap readily available information and make the right decisions about whom they compete against.

What to Look For

Accurately identifying whom a company competes against and then deciding how well you can compete against them therefore requires a fairly comprehensive search for information. It is not enough to find out a competitor's financials — which is the level of effort many companies apply — since this really tells you very little. How did they achieve those financials? What are their costs? What strategies are they using?

Who are their customers? How long have they served these customers? Who are their ex-customers? How long have their employees been with them? What special expertises do the competitors enjoy?

Looking for the information to correctly define competition can come from many directions and all need to be tapped.

Just how extensive this needs to be is demonstrated by the case of a baby soap manufacturer, planning to launch a new version of one of its products. Rather than believe it had all the answers — the company had been making soaps for over a century — an initiative was set up to learn more about competition and the market.

To get the full picture, a series of questions was asked: Who else makes baby soap? How many sizes are available? What strategies are used for reaching new parents? What role do hospitals and doctors play in advising new parents about baby hygiene? What advertising avenues are available? Who manages direct marketing lists of new parents? What co-op marketing or similar initiatives are the competitors using? What are their sales of baby soap products?

Where the Information Came From

Information to answer these questions came from a variety of sources, most in the public domain. Magazines aimed at new parents were sourced and scanned. Hospital staff were interviewed. The Welcome Wagon organization was identified as a key distribution channel. Central purchasers at drugstore chains provided information. List brokers contributed. Finding information on the topic of baby soap became something of a "snowball," gathering momentum and size as new layers of information were added and sources already identified led to even more.

In the case of the Detroit automobile manufacturers referenced in Chapter 3, the answers they didn't have could have been readily enough obtained. Information about the political situation in the Middle East and the relative influence or otherwise of customer nations for oil, such as the U.S., gave some of the early warning signs that the producers might close ranks and make people's lives a bit difficult. The level of non-OPEC sources of oil along with the likely readiness of reserves under exploration and development gave other indicators. Given that the barometer was swinging in the direction it was before the oil crisis hit should have caused someone in Detroit to sit up and say: "Hey! There won't be enough gas!" Or "Gas might become very pricey in North America."

How to deal with this situation was also in the public domain; gas prices in the U.K., Europe, Japan, and other countries have long been, and still are, considerably higher than in the U.S. The know-how, that it was possible, long before the oil crisis, to build lighter, more fuel efficient cars, was available to anyone who bothered to look for it. But that meant going to "someone else's answers", something the Big 3 didn't believe they needed to do.

In the case of the tobacco companies, all they need to do today is conduct patent searches, all information in the public domain, to get the drift of where new competition will likely come from in the future. The increasing use of acupuncture, laser therapy or hypnosis to treat nicotine addiction is well documented in advertisements in alternative health magazines. Exclaiming later — such as 10 years from now — that they didn't see the new competition coming will only indicate that they didn't bother to look.

What is the Payoff from Better Competitive Decisions?

Correctly identifying competition opens the door to a host of better decisions in all areas of the company. Rather than having a direct impact on employees, shareholders, management and other constituents, making accurate decisions about competitors and competitive forces tends to have a payoff in expenditure control or increased profits.

Better expenditure control comes from knowing where the company should increase or decrease its outlay on advertising, promotional activities, new equipment and more in the face of who competitors are and what they are doing. Increased profits come from making such expenditures count; if competitors turn out to be small, under-funded players, then an expenditure on large-scale image ads may not make sense. A better use of the funds may come from investing more in direct marketing to existing customers.

Who Benefits?

If employees do not benefit directly, they certainly benefit indirectly. Making the correct decisions about competitors allows for the sales force to be correctly supported and directed, ditto the customer service reps. and any after-sales service technicians.

Those in charge of operations or production also benefit indirectly when competition decisions are correct. With the "who" of the competition known, the "how" of how competitors run their operations can be determined, providing guidelines for better cost control.

Identifying substitutes, alternates and similar competitive forces, in addition to specific competitors, also provides a better yardstick for a range of management decisions, ranging from acquisitions, divestitures and market entries on down to customer retention strategies.

Checklist	5.8

Questions about competition
- Who do our customers consider to be our competitors?
- Who do our distribution channels consider to be our competitors?
- Who do our suppliers consider to be our competitors?
- What substitutes or alternates represent a source of competition?

- What factors originating in spheres of government, public policy, the legal or regulatory environment constitute a source of competition?
- Which companies were once but no longer are our competitors? Why did they exit the market?
- Which offshore companies could enter our markets and become competitors?

Questions about individual competitors

- Who really owns our competitors?
- How well financed are they?
- What is their scope of operations?
- Which markets and customers do they serve?
- Who are their ex-customers? Why did they leave?
- What are their market strategies?
- What is their sales force like?
- Who handles their advertising?
- Where do they have their operations?
- What are their costs?
- How do they achieve these costs?
- How do they set their prices?
- Who are their employees?
- Which unions represent their workers?
- What expertise do they enjoy that we don't?
- How long have their employees been with them?
- Who are their suppliers?
- How exclusive are these suppliers to our competitors?

Questions about competitive forces

- Which new products or technologies could displace us?
- What changes in legislation or government policy could disrupt or destroy our business?
- What trends developing today could eradicate our markets?
- Which demographic shifts pose a threat to our business?

But Will They Buy? Decisions About New Product Launches

Much like the decision to enter a new market or to diversify, companies which want to grow their business and cannot see opportunities with existing products start looking for new products they can introduce. This might also come about when existing products have reached the end point of their life cycle and must be replaced with new offerings. Launching new products can also be driven by changes in the marketplace such as the aging of the population or a shift in the type of customer demands.

How New Product Launches Happen

In theory, new product launches are the result of long-term, carefully thought-out planning. A company carefully and continually tracks trends to pick up on new directions and new ideas which are emerging. A company will canvass a range of demographic, socio-economic and life style changes and talk to its customers frequently. The objectives of talking to customers are to spot unmet needs and unfilled niches, particularly when customers themselves may not realize they are missing some item or other. Another approach to new product development is to find out how customers actually use what they purchase.

This is the way a company which made fishing tackle boxes discovered that its boxes had uses above and beyond their original purpose. Seamstresses used them for sewing supplies, children used them to organize small toys or art work supplies, models used them to organize makeup. This led to the introduction of similarly designed boxes but made in plastic instead of metal and available in bright colors, which became known as Caboodles. This is an example of a successful new product launch which was based on finding out how purchasers were using the product.

In practice, many new product launches do not follow such a careful trajectory. Often, someone at the company, usually a senior executive, gets a pet idea in mind and Old Demon Ego starts making all the decisions. If the boss is convinced the idea is good, staff lower down very rarely have the authority or the willingness to question the boss and so everyone plunges ahead. Not all unsound new product launches are the result of a single individual however; such initiatives may well come from a group of people who decide a new product should be introduced except in these cases, it is often more a case of people thinking they have all the answers which is driving the decision making.

Whatever the causes of new product failure, however, the rate is still too high; 9 out of 10 new products are said to flop, all of which suggests there is considerable scope for improving how decisions in this sphere of business life are made.

What Gets Forgotten

Probably, some of the better new product ideas are similar to the Caboodles example and owe their success to the fact that some alternate use was already being made of a product. Other new products may be the happy outcome of a mistake; Post-It Notes® from 3M were the result of a failed adhesive, intended for other purposes, but which was found to perfectly suit the objective of posting a temporary note on a page, a calendar, or a fax. Other than these cases, many successful new products involve a grass roots effort or someone close to the end-use to identify the need and come up with the product. This is true of white-out, used for correcting typewritten material, which was developed by a secretary.

But many companies do not operate from these principles when identifying and then launching new products. An example of this was New Coke®, which was almost a case of product by committee decision making; while it was perfectly feasible to introduce a different flavor or variety of Coke, someone forgot to ask the customers how they would feel if the existing product was taken away from them. The resulting new product launch was a corporate catastrophe for Coca Cola.

In the case of Johnson & Johnson, the decision to enter the disposable diaper business was made by a group of managers in the company's consumer products division. The logic, at the surface, cannot be questioned; the company already had some very successful baby care products. But not enough questions — or perhaps the wrong questions — were asked. One of the overlooked factors was the extent to which disposable diapers are really a commodity these days whereas Johnson & Johnson's existing products were strongly branded with a high value-added proposition for consumers. Someone forgot to ask: A new baby-care product, yes, but why diapers?

Exploring markets and identifying customer needs by investing in information gathering can lead to a better new product or the correct positioning of a new product. This was the experience of a small company which had landed exclusive North American rights to a Swedish line of shaving products. One of the products was especially designed to combat pseudofolliculitis, a condition of in-grown hairs which particularly plagues males of Hispanic and African descent.

Two questions came immediately to the minds of the owners of the distribution company: Was there an existing product for pseudofolliculitis? And what were the best avenues to reach the target market?

Extensive research was therefore undertaken to identify any product which was already available (while finding out if not, why not) while uncovering suitable advertising channels to reach the target market. Published information was minimal, even in medical journals, although the problem of pseudofolliculitis runs close to being a medical condition. Trips were made to beauty and barbershop supply outlets along with visits to drugstores and salons in neighborhoods heavily populated by the target groups.

After much scouring of such locations, two products which presented some solution for pseudofolliculitis were unearthed. Rather than being bad news for the distributor, this lack of information presented good news: the market did exist, it had not been correctly developed and the opportunity for them was substantial.

Their new product, if correctly marketed, was slated for good growth.

Anatomy of an Ideal New Product Launch

In an ideal situation, companies which successfully launch many new products are those which are not afraid to try and then have failures, although they realize the failures are such before they are launched on the market. Exploring numerous possibilities for new products is therefore one of the key steps but equally important is keeping in touch with both customers and prospective customers to determine their needs, how they are using existing products and to ferret out unmet needs they have. A key way to do this, of course, is listen to comments such as: If only there was.... Finding out about situations where the customer would like to be able to put out their hand and reach for something — except the something doesn't exist — is a critical way of identifying new product opportunities. But many companies do not want to invest this heavily in obtaining the information to point up these opportunities.

That upfront investment to shape new products or services is worthwhile is demonstrated in the case of a gas utility which decided it wanted to introduce a home energy-audit service, fee-based. Consumer sensitivity to home heating costs varies, not just by time of year but also by the state of the economy; when times are good, people don't worry so much about what their gas or electricity bills look like. The utility therefore wanted to know if home energy audits would provide an enduring line of business. Who else provided them? Were these audits fee-based or free? How were they sold and provided?

Research — which cost only a few thousand dollars — quickly revealed that home energy audits had a checkered history at best. Within the gas utility's service territory, several electrical utilities had abandoned the marketplace while remaining players had switched to a write-in questionnaire, which homeowners filled out and sent in, as opposed to on-site home inspection. Other competition came from services which analyzed all aspects of the home — safety, insulation, fire hazards — not just energy expenditures.

What this told the gas utility was that either they should abandon this avenue of new profit center creation or, they should find ways to position a fee-based option so that it would be attractive to homeowners. Had they not invested in finding out the "lay of the land", they might have launched an inappropriate product in the marketplace and suffered embarrassment, not to mention financial losses, as a result. The information obtained gave them a compass for going forward on a better footing.

What to Look For

What to look for, when deciding about new product initiatives, can be as varied as the proposed products themselves. For a manufacturer of compact fluorescent lightbulbs, looking at a market launch back in the early 1980s, the key question became: Is the market ready? Do people really see that they have high energy cost problems they need to solve? The answer to these questions, and others, came back "Yes" in the United States but "No" in neighboring Canada, where electricity costs have always been lower.

In the case of the Pepsi-Cola six pack, which was more a case of new packaging, the company forgot to look at just how different two markets can be, even when they are only a few hundred miles apart. The factors to determine whether the launch would be successful in Ontario, or if it should even occur, did not stem from competitive activities nor from customer preferences but from the regulatory climate.

Where the Information Came From

As alluded to earlier there was plenty of information Johnson & Johnson could have tapped in the public domain to understand the commodity nature of the diaper business, the requirements of running a paper business, and the likely success rate the company could enjoy. Articles, reports, government studies, plus expert sources at associations, government, retired employees of the other players in the industry could all have been tapped. Ironically, they likely were but another information-related trap into which decision-makers readily fall is only reading what they want to see. Articles which extol the successes of existing players and discuss revenue levels, which sound healthy, may also contain nuggets of wisdom about cost control issues in the industry or describe shrinking margins, but these are conveniently ignored, in favor of the positives.

In the case of the new roasted chicken Tyson Foods introduced, a certain amount of information was available in public domain sources — articles in the trade press, papers given at conferences — but most was only available from the actual trade customers. But, usually, such sources are only too happy to contribute, if and when approached, because it is in their interest to do so.

One of the main theses of this book is that most of the information needed to make better decisions is readily available, whether from customers, as in the case of Tyson Foods, or from good old fashioned leg work, as in the case of products for pseudofolliculitis, which were found during store and barbershop visits. The same was true of information about home energy audits. Articles and even Internet material were scarce so the researchers working on the project volunteered their homes to undergo a series of visits from providers of home energy audits, in this way acting as "guinea pigs." This allowed them to experience first-hand the competing "product" which was, after all, in the public domain.

What is the Payoff from Better New Product Decisions?

At a very superficial level, one of the payoffs of making better decisions about new products is avoiding seeing your company's mistakes displayed at one of the museums of failed products which dot the landscape!

At a deeper level, there is the payoff from ensuring resources are directed into areas where there will be a return on investment. Given that expenditures on products which don't work out run quite high — as in the case of Johnson & Johnson's failed diaper — any company will be better off in the long run, if it can weed out the duds sooner rather than later in the process. Information is readily available to help do this in many cases; the best time to gather it is while the new product is in what's termed the "conceptual stage" before raw materials are bought, before machines are re-tooled, before space has been leased for the development of the new product.

If a company can avoid such expenditures on products which are destined for the scrap heap and only make them on the surer bets, then the payoff of better new product decisions will go straight to the bottom line.

Who Benefits?

While it might seem less obvious, customers are one of the main beneficiaries of better new product decisions, not just because the products which are launched will meet more of their needs but because such products are sustainable. Customers do not take kindly to finding products they are using either pulled from the shelves, because the market was too small or the company could not go on manufacturing it for some reason or other. Customers also do not want to see older products they are currently using withdrawn because a company's new product ventures are so unsuccessful that financial difficulties necessitate a rationalization of the entire existing product line.

Checklist   5.9

Questions about new product direction

- How are our customers using our current products? Are these the uses for which the product was intended?
- If it is an alternate use, is it legal and does it represent a broader opportunity for us?
- How can our existing products be modified to serve new markets?
- What will be the impact of any new product on our existing lines? Will sales of the new product cannibalize sales from other areas?
- Where are the gaps in our existing product line? How can we fill them?
- What new products are our competitors working on?
- What new technologies, substances, products, or designs are currently being patented?
- How can we capitalize on them?
- What products or technologies are available for license?
- What research is being done outside our company, such as at universities, which offers new product opportunities for us?

Questions about new products

- Why this particular product? What other options were considered?
- If this product doesn't yet exist or is not made by someone else, why not?
- What might demand be for the new product?
- Will it have international appeal or does it just suit our domestic market?
- If it is for our domestic market, is the appeal local, regional or national?
- Will our customers really buy it (as opposed to just saying they will)?
- If this product is not intended for our existing customer base, who are the intended customers?
- How do we go about finding them?
- How can we protect this product via patents or other channels?
- What competition might emerge for this new product? How quickly will competitors be able to imitate us?
- How might such competition affect demand for our product?
- How will we distribute this product? Can we use existing channels or do we need to look for new ones?
- Who can supply the inputs we need? Who owns these suppliers? Is there an open market for the inputs?
- Where can we test market the new product?

Selected References

"Defining Your Competition," in *Competitive Intelligence Review,* (various issues).

"Flops," *Business Week,* April 16, 1993, pp. 76–80, 82.

"Have You Taken Your Nullo Today?" *Globe & Mail,* March 14, 1998, p. D15.

"Heart and Head," *Marketing,* March 1998, p. 34.

"How to Cash in on Frustration," *Globe & Mail,* September, 12, 1998.

"Knowing Rivals' Costs Clear Profit Picture," *Globe & Mail,* April 10, 1998, p. B19.

"Lost in Space at Boeing," *Business Week,* April 27, 1998, p. 42.

"Study: Glamor Megamergers Fall Short in the Long Run," *Purdue News,* June 1998, p 1.

"The Shanghai Bubble," *Forbes,* April 20, 1998, p. 48.

"Would You Spend $1.50 for a Razor Blade?" *Business Week,* April 27, 1998, p. 46.

6 Protecting Your Career with the Right Decisions

"In a time of turbulence and change,
it is more true than ever that knowledge is power"
John F. Kennedy, 1962

What does all this mean for you personally? If you are currently employed by a business organization — or any organization — how can you apply this to protect and enhance your career?

The answer to this will depend on the organization you work for, its people and politics, its size and the nature of the industry you're in. But regardless of these factors, there are still likely many ways you can take action to improve the information available to support decisions and thus the quality of the decisions made. Whether the steps taken are small or large is not the point; the fact they are taken is.

What this can involve is no more than remaining alert to information, broadening your understanding of what a source of information is and where it might come from, learning how to organize for information work and how to work efficiently through a lot of data, when the need arises. Being a better user of information in decision making may also mean becoming more aware of the different methodologies available to conduct research and the strengths and weaknesses of these different methodologies, as applied to the various types of decision which have to be made.

And what if the company you work for remains obdurate, refusing to mend its ways? The signs suggest that such a company will not survive the information-intensive era of the 21st century and will likely fold. If your colleagues and superiors really seem determined to close their ears and their minds, it might be time to consider changing jobs.

Better Information Equals Better Decisions

Anyone who has lived through consequences of poor decision making such as losing their job in a downsizing, being forced to relocate and then relocate again as company plans change, seeing business opportunities missed due to lack of money, etc., probably doesn't need convincing that better decisions are often needed in the workplace. Or, that any existing practices for making decisions which do turn out to be good ones should be kept up.

Having read the preceding chapters, the role of information — having the right information at the right time — as the foundation of good decision making, should be firmly established. The next step is to make the commitment to better decision making a part of everyday business life.

Putting Information on the Agenda

Such a commitment should be corporate-wide at every company, but many individuals will find themselves working in an environment where such an orientation does not exist. That means the person in this situation has to take on a double role: ensuring their own decisions are the right ones, supported by the right information, and finding ways to raise the level of understanding in the work environment to encourage everyone to follow in the same path.

One of the first steps is to identify which individuals, at all levels of the organization, already value information and see its role as crucial in decision making. Some of the hallmarks of such individuals are: they likely read extensively and seek out information in this way; they likely travel out of choice, for their vacations, and venture further afield than their own backyard; they likely work in departments where obtaining information from both inside and outside the company is a part of life. Purchasing may be one such department, marketing and sales should be another. But don't confine an informal survey of information use to the obvious; engineering, production and logistics may equally be areas where colleagues will already recognize the value of information to support decision making.

Once identified, colleagues can join as part of an informal network or act as champions of the process.

Keeping a Log

One of the better ways to "raise consciousness" in the organization is to keep a log of decisions that have been made and their consequences. Rather than undertake this exercise as a witch hunt, it should be undertaken in the spirit of "let's do it better next time," with no blame attached. For example: "Remember when we switched suppliers three months ago and found the quality of products wasn't high enough? For this upcoming supplier decision, I suggest we formulate some different questions and have the answers before we make our choice."

Another tactic is to keep a history or log of how other companies went wrong, by not using information as a basis for decision making. The advantage of looking elsewhere and collecting such stories is that, when you bring them out, everyone can laugh at them but still learn from the process. For example: "Remember how Competitor A ended up with that 'white elephant' warehouse over in the next county where taxes are three times as high as here?" (wait for laughter) "Here's how we can avoid the same mistake. The key questions they *didn't* answer are...."

Tactics to Use with Peers

Developing a role as the person who can come up with the right questions — the underpinning of all good information-based decisions — and willingly assisting co-workers with this task, ensures that your efforts will be seen positively and in a non-threatening light. Becoming known as a resource person, someone who can always generate a good range of questions, will enhance your role as a team-player and create positive visibility for your career.

Another tactic to use with peers is to encourage discussion about non-business decisions which they feel comfortable discussing. Most people are willing to share horror stories — as well as good experiences — from their personal lives: car and house buying, selecting a travel agent or a stockbroker, how they went about finding a good doctor or dentist following a relocation. These will all provide a springboard for looking at the role of information and how did they gather input, how did they evaluate it, what would they do differently next time. Such discussions naturally throw a spotlight on how information was a "make or break" factor, and will lead to common ground for the support you need to put information — or more information — into the decision-making process at work.

Tactics to Use with Superiors

When it comes to nudging superiors along the path of better decision making, tactic might be less an appropriate word than tact; executives who commit any of the seven deadly sins of decision making outlined in Chapter 3 of this book might not take very kindly to having the weak link in their thinking exposed.

Here again, it's useful to have a log book of examples, notably positive ones from the company's history, when the right decisions were taken. Even if the executives currently at the company were not in on those decisions, most of the time they will be happy to bask in the glow of what turned out to be an excellent choice. Suggest that current decisions on the table can be equally positive with an input of such and such information and then steer the process in a favorable direction. It can be equally effective to use negative examples from other companies, especially competitors, showing how not to make decisions. Few executives at your own company will want to be guilty of making the same sort of blunders and are therefore more likely to be persuaded of the importance of good information as a foundation for any decisions they have to make.

Another equally useful tactic with superiors is developing and then describing two or three different outcomes from the decision at hand. Such scenarios can be varied but still plausible enough to raise doubts in peoples' minds as to which might be the outcome and will prompt them to take the necessary steps to ensure information is obtained to narrow down the range of possibilities to the most positive outcome and thereby indicate which decision should be made.

Alternatively, if the decisions to be made can't be framed in terms of outcomes just yet, try presenting two puzzles or problems in need of resolution. Make them intriguing enough but alarming enough to engage the serious attention of your executives, while ensuring your superior won't be able to fire an answer off the top of his or her head. Involve the executive in deciding which problem to probe further, to ensure their "buy-in". For example, if you have discovered a competitor has re-routed all their delivery routes so they are now longer and, in theory, more costly and, at the same time, the competitor has set up a special sales force to target your key accounts, present both problems and have your executive or manager decide which is more important to investigate.

Tactics to Use with Subordinates

Working with those who report to you is probably less of a mine field when it comes to steering decision making in the direction of an information-based model. Subordinates may actually seek your guidance from time to time; if you encourage the kind of creative thinking that leads to good analysis of a problem situation, you will soon stimulate them to come up with the right questions to shape further information gathering exercises. Collective brainstorming efforts are one way to go about this, with the resulting questions pooled and regrouped to form the basis for further information gathering or research.

When looking to subordinates for input into decision making, don't assume by position titles or functions filled that people don't have ideas. Those who sometimes say very little and may more correctly be termed "observers" at the company may actually be better able to pull together more information in their heads than those who might be termed "movers and shakers." Observers are sometimes like sponges, absorbing information from multiple sources; these are often the people who notice what the customers are doing and can see patterns, or notice what's going on in the marketplace and notice trends. Your role in encouraging good decision making should be to involve these people and tap their observations.

Developing a Process

Organizations which tend to make good decisions most of the time usually have a process to guide information gathering and decision making. This usually involves identifying the magnitude of the decision and then having some guidelines or structure as to who needs to be involved in the decision and how much external validation is required.

For example, making a decision about a new contractor for the company cafeteria may not involve as long or rigorous a decision-making process as selecting a contractor to build the company's new warehouse and distribution center. In the case of the cafeteria, the infrastructure (counters, hot plates, ovens, etc.) may already be in place, meaning a provider of food and attendant services is all that is sought. Since it is relatively easy to go and see other sites the supplier is operating and relatively easy to see how they're serving you once the contract has been signed (although this still represents gathering information to support the decision), the impact on the long-term health of your organization is not as potentially severe as with the choice of an engineering firm to put up the warehouse. In the case of the cafeteria, the contract may also be for a one- or two-year period and easier to terminate prior to completion if things don't work out; with the warehouse and distribution center, the immediate financial implications of a poor contractor choice, never mind the longer term environmental and cost impacts, are far greater.

This suggests effective decision making needs to be based on an agreed-upon process: how much information to gather, from whom, reviewed by which departments, and so on. This process should actually be tiered, to allow for different degrees of information gathering and vetting, prior to the final decision being made.

Cutting a Process Down to Size

In contrast, some organizations have too much of a process; too many people are involved, too many viewpoints influence the final outcome, as shown in "Decision Drag" in Chapter 3. If this is the situation at your organization, you may want to find ways to streamline the process. Naturally, knowing the people and politics is essential. However, there are likely individuals who are on the "circulation list" for decisions they have little interest in and actually find a nuisance. The best tactic here is to approach them from the perspective of their time and how much time could be freed up by only involving them in the decisions which genuinely affect them or to which they should be contributing.

Do Your Homework — Then Act

In many situations, your role at work may be to contribute to the analysis of a situation and to generate questions but when it does fall to your lot to follow through and actually guide the information gathering and decision making process, there may be a moment or two when the task seems overwhelming, particular when you first tackle something like this.

After all your initiatives, "preaching" etc., the company has finally listened to you and wants your more active participation. At times such as this, it's probably a good idea to go back to first principles a bit. Re-read parts of this book. Or, review your log or history book. Define the desired outcomes. Generate a list of pros and cons for the decision under consideration.

Getting Started

One of the better starting points, even if you do not know yet whether an outside research supplier will be used or not, is to draft a Request for Proposal (RFP) or otherwise develop some guidelines. Itemize all the things you would want an outside supplier to investigate; also itemize the decisions which have to be taken once the information has been gathered. Remember, whether you end up gathering information or going outside, that such an RFP is not graven in stone but needs to be modified or "tweaked" in the light of information which the research process turns up.

For example, if a new market entry is to be made, create a list of all the positives which would suggest going ahead and then on another list all the negatives, all the bad things which could happen to make the market entry an unsound decision. Formulate questions or hypotheses that must be tested to weigh "both sides of the coin". If the growth rate in the market looks attractive, then what are the factors which are contributing to this? How long have they been present in the marketplace? And what could change those factors, removing them from the picture?

Keys to Key Questions

If you do have trouble coming up with questions readily, then develop a system for generating them. Down the left hand side of a page or on your computer screen, put the seven key words that start most of the questions human beings ask: Why? What? When? Where? How? Who? Which? Then see how many questions you can generate, relevant to the topic, beginning with each of these words. Why is the market growing? What could change it? When might this occur? etc. Alternatively, review the questions listed in Chapter 5 of this book and use these as a springboard to more.

Note that you will not ask the same questions to support each and every decision that comes along but must formulate new ones tailor-made to the situation at hand. That is why another time, your questions might well go:

Which companies are exiting the market? What is making them do this? When will they be getting out? How does this change the opportunity for us?

As discussed many times throughout this book, making a better decision rests on having the right information and enough of it. Getting enough of the right information rests on asking the right questions at the start of the process. Not asking the right questions or — more importantly — not allowing them onto the agenda once the research process is underway, is the reason most people end up making bad decisions.

Selecting Outside Suppliers

If yours is a company which actually encourages the use of outside suppliers in the information gathering process and sets aside budgets for this purpose, it is important to maximize the situation to your advantage. When funds permit, always take the opportunity to assign research to more than one supplier, either to have them tackle a problem from different angles or to provide complementary analysis of a particular situation. (Direct, parallel overlap might not always be a good idea; if the range of expert sources is limited, such sources might not appreciate being phoned and interviewed by two or three suppliers in quick succession).

Before even selecting a supplier, however, it is a good idea to present the situation in enough detail to provide a full picture and find out how the suppliers would tackle the question. Trying to control the process too closely or spelling out where this supplier should look for information, will only produce "step 'n' fetchit" results. As much as possible, you want to work with suppliers who can provide more input and value-added results than that.

Finding out about the range of problems suppliers have tackled in the past and how successful they have been with coming up with information is one way of evaluating potential suppliers. When discussing your present situation, notice which suppliers ask the best questions and the most questions. Just because a supplier is raising objections, doesn't mean that he or she is not suited to the task. Often, such objections are born of experience in the field and may indicate to you where your own approach to the research might not produce the results you want.

Strengths and Limitations

Key to successful supplier selection is knowing the strengths and weaknesses of each method used. If you turn to internal libraries or external consultancies staffed by those with library training, then the methodologies offered may rely heavily on bibliographic and database sources and provide secondary research only. Research firms which specialize in searches under the Freedom of Information Legislation will likely tap just government files. Firms employing investigative journalists or private investigators will conduct research that is more slanted towards primary research. Then, companies which do structured phone surveys or use focus groups heavily may only have experience doing consumer research as opposed to business-to-business research. Other firms may be "full service" and offer a combination of all these methods.

A Second Opinion

As mentioned above, it's also beneficial to get two or more independent parties to conduct research to answer the questions formulated. This doesn't mean that you don't gather information yourself but the rule of thumb is: the more important or expensive the decision to be made (as gauged by the dollar amounts involved in either going ahead with something or avoiding it all together), the more outside objectivity is required.

It's also key here to make sure outside counsel is objective. Consultants you work with frequently may try to second-guess your intentions. Firms which work exclusively in your industry may make assumptions too often rather than conducting actual original research. You will need to study what is required from each supplier. Is it technical expertise? Or market expertise? Or, is it a particular approach to information gathering or an approach to analysis of the results that will make a difference in the situation at hand?

Certain types of decisions will require a consultant or firm who has done the exact type of work before. In other situations, such as when markets are stagnating or demand for a long time product has stalled, you may need input from someone who will look for new answers and be more creative and come up with more off-beat solutions, than someone who works regularly in the industry. Where companies often sabotage the information contribution to decision making is when they hire consultants who will tell them what they want to hear, is discussed in the section on "Hear No Evil." In these situations, the word "trusted" takes on a new twist; the "trusted" advisors won't go outside the company's comfort zone and the truth will either be diluted or sugar coated or worse, hidden all together.

Caveat Emptor

Even when you are sure you have the right supplier, if it is the first time you have worked with them, be aware of some of the events which go on behind the scenes. Determining if your research supplier has a permanent staff or merely ships people in and out, as needed, will tell you about continuity within the firm's work and how stable they are. If the staff aren't permanent, there may not be any retention of experience or learning from assignment to assignment, a key point if you expect to work with the supplier again.

This means it is also critical to find out what and how often the supplier subcontracts. Will all the work for your assignment be done in one place? Or will it be farmed out, across the country or perhaps around the globe? In this latter case, is this a positive or a negative, relative to your objectives? If you happen to be gathering information to support a critical and highly confidential decision, no matter how your main supplier assures you secrets will be kept and no matter how many pieces of paper they sign to that effect, the fact is, the more diluted the control, the more likely there will be a leak.

Be aware, as well, of the fact that some information suppliers, rather than conducting the original, custom research you have contracted for, may actually be about to re-gurgitate work done for someone else and palm it off on you. You may be paying several thousands of dollars for what you believe is countless hours of labor when all they are doing is changing client references in a document and re-jigging some of the text or numbers to suit you.

When You Must Do-it-Yourself

Sometimes a lack of budgets and other resources mean that you are going to have to undertake information gathering to support decision making yourself. Until they have actually tried it, many people actually think finding information is something of a "plum" job meaning people actually jockey for such opportunities in large companies. As anyone who has actually gone out and gathered information can tell you, it is very rarely a straightforward and simple process; many is the person who, after three days of spinning their wheels, finds that they are no further ahead in the information they need to gather. Do-it-yourselfers frequently commit the last of the seven deadly sins, namely, thinking good things come to those who wait; they truly believe that if they just do nothing and wait long enough, the exact information they need will drop into their lap. This is rarely going to be the case and probably only happens in 5% of information gathering exercises. The first thing to do, when you must do research yourself, is to allow enough time to get your feet wet and get up to speed in the particular topic you are investigating. There are some industries which, for various reasons, do not need to advertise or publicize very much and where everyone knows everyone else. If you are an outsider trying to learn about this industry, you will find it very tough to get any information. The same will be true for very new industries which do not yet have a full infrastructure of associations, directories, government departments regulating them, etc.; finding information about ventures in such industries will also be very time-consuming.

To avoid the trap of finding out only what you want to hear, you need to play different roles with yourself to create a framework for further information gathering. Generate a list of questions a supporter of the idea would ask and then generate a list of questions a naysayer would ask. Make sure you cover all the angles in the information you gather. Information gathered to support someone's pet project or a particular point of view runs the risk of producing a bad decision.

Remember that sources lead to sources; if you systematically go through what is available in the way of information, if you look within this information you will probably find the avenues to more. Always ask everyone you speak to if they have another source to recommend or know of someone else you should speak with. This is often how you find out the real information, especially when the topic is highly competitive or highly secretive in nature.

Action Speaks Louder Then Words

Once the information is all in and if it truly, really does provide the foundation for a decision (beware of question migration here), then go ahead and make the decision. In cases where you are the ultimate decision maker, this will be the final link in the chain; in cases where you have to have the idea vetted by others in your organization, rather than present them with the research, present them with a recommendation backed by the research (but always remember to keep this decision making support, in case someone wants to see it later).

He or She who Hesitates — Too Much — Loses Their Job

A little hesitation can be good for the soul but too much can be deadly. In an earlier chapter, we discussed the fact that no decision can be as lethal as the wrong decision. That's why all business decision makers need to strike a balance between enough hesitation (which allows time for some information gathering) and too much hesitation (which may lead to an unresolved mess which ends up costing you your job).

Once you have been asked to be involved in a decision — or if making decisions is part of your job anyway — getting on with it is the best way to keep your job.

Understanding Your Own Style

Knowing your own decision making style is essential to balancing out any weaknesses: are you a risk-taker, a risk-avoider, or somewhere in between?

If you tend to be a "shoot first, ask questions later" kind of decision maker, then you need to balance out your style by allowing for an information-gathering process.

This means recognizing you may be particularly prone to "fly-by-the-seat-of-your-pants" decisions, to believing you have all the answers, to listening to the whisperings of Old Demon Ego. In such cases, it may be best to always seek some kind of external support for decision making as doing it yourself may lead you into the temptation of short-circuiting the process, of migrating your questions to suit information which comes easily to hand.

If on the other hand, you tend to delay decisions or procrastinate, it is important to balance this out by obtaining information but not to the extent where information-gathering becomes an excuse or a delaying tactic. An honest assessment may show you to be liable to committing the "Hurry Up and Wait" sin of decision making or, perhaps, to committing that of asking the wrong questions to derail the process deliberately, so you can spend even more time gathering information.

Then again, if you are a resolute Do-It-Yourselfer for just about everything, you need to assess how this style may jeopardize any decisions you make at work. Apart from believing you have all the answers, you may also fall victim to the jumping on the bandwagon style of decision making, as this can become the line of least resistance. Making use of others in the decision making process, whether internal resources or external suppliers, may be a wise move to balance out your style.

Master delegators, on the other hand, probably need to balance out their style by learning a little more about the information gathering process and the different methodologies their research suppliers, whether internal or external, use. Delegators may be especially vulnerable to committing the sin of Hearing No Evil, due to their desire to distance themselves from the process. Becoming slightly more involved will provide a safety valve.

The Price of Procrastination

Companies, and the people who work for them, who end up with a bad decision on their hands often end up this way because they hesitated too long. It can be something relatively simple; an oil drip from machine which should have been fixed but wasn't, because no one wanted to decide to call in a specialist to check it over (because that would cost money) ends up creating a puddle which causes someone to slip, leading to a lawsuit.

When people hesitate over such simple decisions, it isn't surprising they hesitate even more over the larger ones. This is where the deadly sin of "saving" money comes in to play; some people believe that by avoiding an investment in information to make their decisions, the problem will maybe work itself out or go away and they won't even have to make any decision. Such an approach to decision making bears a heavy price tag, much heavier than financing the effort to find valuable information, tailored information, which always takes time. Such a level of effort is not as easy as doing nothing.

Beating procrastination involves simply getting started; once the information gathering process has started, it is always possible to stop and review the results and then redirect if necessary. Anyone with a tendency to procrastinate on gathering information for decision making needs to set themselves targets and, if necessary, rewards for completing these milestones.

Fear of Information

Another reason people procrastinate on gathering information is fear; fear of what the information might say. If a decision to divest a subsidiary or exit a market is on the table, there's a strong possibility that certain individuals — including those doing the investigating — may well lose their jobs. This phenomenon is closely tied to another of the seven deadly sins, namely, we already have all the answers. One of the reasons people cling to the notion that they already know all the answers is they are truly afraid of what a fresh input of information might tell them.

As discussed, in the case of the Canadian seminar company, fear of actually acting upon the information was likely the real driver of excuses about paying bills or imaginings about the deliverables. In this way, procrastination is part of a vicious circle: the company procrastinates on getting the information so it won't have to make the decision for fear of what the next steps would be if it did get the information and made the decision.

Analysis Paralysis

At the opposite end of the spectrum are those people who get started on gathering information right away and do so furiously until they have mounds of it, and then spend forever refining their analysis. This approach is really another form of procrastination and a very clever one at that; no-one can accuse such individuals of not doing their job and they can always blame the overabundance of information as a reason they cannot bring their decision making to any resolution.

In fact, there are ways to deal with this problem. With any research process, you have to have certain milestones or even a final cutoff, which can be suggested naturally from the information gathering process itself. Setting milestones by the information gathering process itself rather than by the calendar is preferable, simply because calendar-set deadlines don't always allow for how difficult it sometimes is to turn up information that with persistence and a longer timeframe can be found. When a decision is truly critical to the success of a company, allowing enough time to gather information is essential provided this timeframe does not become a crutch for avoiding making the decision.

Reaching Milestones

Certain stages of the information gathering process do suggest milestones for completion. One is when you reach the point of diminishing returns; when you have truly found all recently published documents and there are no more turning up from searches. Another such milestone is reached when expert sources are producing a high level of repetition as to what they say and the type of information they are sharing. When such a point is reached there is no real point in going on with a lot more such interviews. Another milestone is reached when the majority of questions raised at the start of the process — plus any which emerged during the information gathering process — have been answered and it is possible to make good guesses at the answers to those which are left. This point might be reached when nine-tenths or more of the questions have been answered by outside sources and independent observation.

Can You Ever Make a Decision with Little or No Information?

Some people might argue that if every decision has to first have a solid base of information, then the wheels of commerce and most other activities in life would grind to a halt. Time marches on and opportunities don't wait, they might argue.

To see if this point of view is valid, consider the many decisions you make each day with seemingly little or no information gathering: Where to park your car, where to eat lunch, where to take your dry cleaning. Obviously, you don't engage in a laborious research process each time you make these decisions. But they are, nevertheless, information-based.

Trial and Error

Before you settled on where to park every day, assuming you pay, you probably scoped out the neighborhood and checked everyone's prices. You know where you can get the sort of lunch you like at a price you want to pay, because you've either tried out a few places in your neighborhood or, when travelling, you eat at national chains you know something about. Ditto the dry cleaner; perhaps you checked with neighbors or colleagues or took "test" garments to different cleaners, before settling on the one you use?

In fact, such everyday decisions are usually heavily information-based; it is just that the research process was either invisible — you had to eat lunch somewhere each day — or is long forgotten. The only humans who probably don't make personal decisions based on some sort of information are very young children who plunge into the unfamiliar before a bad experience makes them shy away. Even then, by the age of two or three, the human memory kicks in and some of the information gathered in the time-honored trial and error research method reminds the toddler of things that bite or sting and are therefore best avoided.

Sensory Input

One of the main ways to decide if you can make a decision without a lot of information is to see if any of your five senses can provide the answers you seek first, before you turn to other sources. If you can use sight, smell, taste, touch or hearing to get immediate input to evaluate a situation, the need for other types of more cerebral or intellectual information, like the information discussed throughout this book, drops off. For example, if you can see a sample of fabric that your company needs or touch it, your need for other information to support a supplier decision may be limited to checking a couple of references. But when it comes to an expansion overseas, such as into the Indonesian market, it is not possible to see or hear or touch all the pros and cons of this market, not even by visiting; there are always going to be aspects of the economy, markets, government regulations and business climate which are neither visible nor audible and for which you need to gather less tangible information in order to make a sound decision.

Many people probably don't perceive their five senses as information-gathering devices but we use them every day for that very purpose. We use our senses to gather information about the weather so we know what the temperature is and how to dress appropriately. Although in the modern era this information can be gathered from radio and television, there is more than one person who still figures out what the weather will do today by looking out at the sky. We use smell to tell if food is good or bad for us, long before we involve our taste sense, so we can inform ourselves as to whether we should eat the food or not. Our sense of sight provides information about the safety of the sidewalk, especially in icy weather, and tells us whether we should walk there or not.

As a result, our five senses are continually picking up information and relaying it to our minds but when the senses can't serve to provide the information we need, we turn to other methods. This is where gathering information of an intellectual or conceptual nature to support business decisions kicks in. In such cases, this information is a sensory input for the brain.

What is Gut Feel?

Of course, there's another natural sense which sometimes plays a role in decision making and that's our sixth sense, more popularly known as gut feel. In the rational, scientific climate of the late 20th century, gut feel has often been held in low regard. Events which cannot be scientifically proven or rationally substantiated tend to be dismissed. At the same time, over-reliance on gut feel can get people into a lot of trouble when it comes to business decision making.

Gut feel refers to a reaction or sensation in the pit of the stomach. Historically, this was a part of the human's sensory armor, the "flight or fight" response. Even today, when a situation may be dangerous — such as wandering down a dark, unlit alley in a strange town — the survival mechanisms in the human body trigger warnings, often sensed as a "gut feeling" in the pit of the stomach.

Are You Really Relying on Gut Feel?

So, how can someone strike a balance between over-relying on gut feel and ignoring it altogether? What are the situations where gut feel won't let you down? Usually, people who say they rely on gut feel to make decisions, really are going on more than this; they already have a lot of other information about a subject or considerable experience but just haven't identified or assessed that they do have this knowledge. Suppose your gut feel tells you you should enter a particular market. This might be a geographic market or a demographic market in which you have never before operated. However, in the case of a geographic market, you may have visited the area repeatedly over a period of time and therefore have built up more knowledge about it than you realize, all of which is prompting you to have the gut feel in the first place. The same is true of a demographic market; perhaps you don't serve a particular age group or earnings group but perhaps you know a lot about them, from either living in a particular area, or hearing about this demographic from others you do business with. Chances are your gut feel is based on more than just what's going on in your stomach. (Even then, subjecting the business idea to some objective information support is still a good idea).

Primeval Practices

Methodologies — if they can even be called that — involving trial and error, sensory input or gut feel as a basis for decision making really hark back to more primitive eras of human development and need to be balanced out.

As research methods or decision guidance systems, they tend to be high-risk. All originated at times when other forms of information were not available.

There are many situations in business where relying just on gut feel will jeopardize a lot of activities. These situations arise when you emotionally want something and are using gut feel to rationalize or kid yourself it will be OK and that the decision is sound. An honest appraisal at times like these will probably quickly identify that you do not have any information or have only insufficient information to go ahead with your plan.

Let's suppose that your gut feel tells you to go ahead and buy a company that you've heard is up for sale. Just because you want to buy the business doesn't mean it's a good idea; this is the business equivalent of the eyes being bigger than the stomach. If, on analysis, you find you really know very little about the business or realize that some of the things you believe are totally incorrect, you will find that your gut feel has nothing to do with prior information and everything to do with an emotion such as greed. Making a decision to purchase the company, under these circumstances, will probably end up bringing a lot of grief into your life.

Likewise, if you like the way an office location looks and decide to lease on the basis of this visual sensory input alone, you may end up in a building with a host of problems. And, no one in business needs to be told the trial-and-error information gathering is not only time-consuming but also highly expensive. Deciding to make acquisitions this way could easily bury an organization.

The Balancing Act

That's why it's better to balance such decisions with some information. Even better, is to gather information not only to support what your gut feel says but also to challenge it, trying to present a contrarian opinion. If the information still turns up in support of going ahead with the decision and purchasing the company, then you will likely be making a sound decision and one that has also moved out of the realm of gut feel and into the realm of being an information-based decision.

Another advantage of balancing out gut feel with some external information is that this may lead you to a better idea. If you have a gut feel about a new product, some customer and marketplace input may refine your concept to lead to an item with a higher margin or a greater profit potential. From a single product idea, external information may lead you to a package concept which offers even greater growth opportunities.

Opportunity Knocks Once

Those who still want to make a case for the information-less decision might take one final run at the issue and say: what about once-in-a-lifetime opportunities which arise? What if you spot a hot new product you want to license? What if you suddenly realize there's a market not being served which you could enter?

The key words to watch for, when such detractors of information-based decision making start talking are, words such as "suddenly" or "spot" or any which imply a discovery has just been made. People who tend to want to live on the edge this way are often those who enjoy the adrenalin surge of a crisis and may even fabricate such crises because they feel so good while they're solving them.

Businesses, no question, need to be able to respond quickly to changes in the marketplace and other developments but, in companies where information-gathering is a way of life, there are hardly any surprises. In Chapter 3, examples of information available today which point the way to the future were given. New uses for tobacco, a mass defection to alternative therapies, impacts from the aging population, changes in climate: all the signs are there now (and are being ignored by many companies which, it is suspected, are really run by adrenalin junkies).

Companies which make the switch to placing even more emphasis on information content to prepare for the business climate of the 21st century are the ones who will face very few surprises. They will be much less likely to be caught off-guard by opportunities which "suddenly" appear; more likely, they will have been watching them emerge and biding their time to seize such opportunities, much like the manufacturer of compact fluorescent light bulbs cited earlier, who entered the U.S. market but waited over five years before launching the same product in Canada. By waiting until the timing was more opportune, they saved themselves the costs of an unsuccessful market entry but still had a product ready to go, which they could ramp up fairly quickly, to be ahead of any competitors.

This suggests that no, you can never make a decision with little or no information and that, in many personal decisions, you don't do this, although the information element has become largely transparent.

Why then do so many companies fail to make use of information in their business decision making? Whatever the reasons, which vary from organization to organization, changes need to be made.

Becoming more information aware and committed to information content means a company is pro-active, unlike the reactive decision makers profiled in Chapter 3. Such an information-oriented organization is one well equipped to use information as a tool and make the right decisions in the coming century.

7

Conclusion: Excellence in Decision Making — The 21st Century Imperative

*"Be not ignorant of any thing
in a great matter or a small"*
Ecclesiasticus (Apocrypha) 5:15

A brief glance at history quickly shows us that no new century is the same as the one that preceded it. Much of the way of life and the belief systems of the 17th century were swept away by the Age of Enlightenment and the revolutions of the 18th century. The mechanical inventions of the 19th century transformed the world until it bore no resemblance to that of the 18th. The new technologies of the 20th century have unraveled much of what was created in the 19th. Therefore, it is fair to predict that whatever develops in the 21st century will dissolve, dissipate or destroy much of what exists in the 20th.

Exactly what those changes will be is hard to predict simply because so many predictions turn out to be wrong. As was mentioned earlier in this book, some of the business-related changes predicted for the coming decades: more self-employment, more leisure time, more virtual corporations, more use of computer networks, are not so likely to come true as the technology gurus would like to have us believe. One of the characteristics of technology lovers which has never been probed is the extent to which they are socioempathic or sociopathic; listening to their rapt discourses on the wonders of fixating on a computer screen for work, play, entertainment, love and more, one can only wonder if these individuals even know any human beings? And, if they do, do they really like them?

The longer track record of human history which transcends nationality, culture and technology, shows a marked tendency, in all parts of the world and all cultures, for people to seek out other people and congregate together. Given the increasing urbanization of much of the planet — the teeming cities of Asia with populations of 15, 20, or 25 million being just one example — the evidence suggests that human beings actually prefer being around other human beings and seeing them face to face. Perhaps not too close, but close, nonetheless. Coupled with the repeated failure of "back to the land" movements, which are not just a phenomenon of the 20th century, and this particular direction of human development does not seem set for a 180 degree turn. A 45 degree turn, perhaps, as people move to smaller urban centers, transit villages and the like, but no immediate abondonment of being too far from one another. This suggests some of the technology-based predictions which proliferated in the late 20th century, will not come true, inherently isolating as they are.

What will come true, is the realization of slower developing trends which are already in motion. Information has always been critical to human endeavor, it has always been the lifeblood of commerce. But whereas historically people took this for granted — the person with the best information usually wins — in the 21st century, becoming not only more aware of information but more pro-active in its use will be mission critical to enterprises large and small.

Even reasonably sophisticated businesses which do pay as much attention, in the late 20th century, to information content as they do to information infrastructure (systems, networks and the like) still leave a lot to chance. In the 21st century, the management of information content will become more critical, the act of deliberately seeking out information more constant, the willingness to invest as heavily in content as in systems more accepted. Without this commitment to information, erstwhile large and successful enterprises will flounder and fail, in that the whole arena of competition will turn on information, with victory going to whoever has the best of it.

Businesses will no longer be able to commit the Seven Deadly Sins in their decision making because the consequences of a misstep will be too catastrophic. Individuals who do not have the skills both in terms of innate attitudes and learned skills to make good decisions will have to be kept away from decision making roles. The emphasis placed on information in the 21st century will be far higher than in the 20th.

Contrary to what some of the technology gurus predict, this emphasis on information will not be satisfied by more and more technology. While it is possible to build such sophisticated networks, to link humans both visually and auditorially miles apart, to store millions of terabytes of information and to perform similar technology feats, there is nothing to suggest that delegating all critical thinking to machines is a good idea.

While it may be possible to develop an "Intelligent Room", one which responds to our verbal commands for information or even volunteering information we hadn't thought of, as is the case with an initiative at MIT's Artificial Intelligence Lab, this is not the same as saying such a move is desirable. The computer made of silicon chips will never replace the one made of neurons and gray matter. Anyone who suggests otherwise should be questioned closely: why do they want to make humans obsolete? Or, at the very most, indolent non-functioning blobs? Is there any place for people in their world? While it may be true that humans are the only species which will fight to the point of self-annihilation, must it also be true that we are the only species designing a world in which we become redundant?

Looking back over the human track record of the last (20th) century alone, it does not take long to see that for every win we scored, we chalked up an equal number of losses. We've all but eradicated diphtheria and smallpox but, at the same time, our hog-wild approach to antibiotic use has led to the emergence of resistant strains of bacteria plus many people with impaired immune function due to the over-prescription of so-called wonder drugs.

We've found ways to reduce the number of traffic fatalities from the days of deathtrap-on-wheels automobiles of the 1950s, but some of our solutions — such as airbags — have proven less than safe. We've cut polluting emissions from cars and from factories but the over-use of chemical fertilizers, pesticides and herbicides has created substandard, polluted soil and led to poorer quality food as a result. From external pollution of the human environment to internal pollution of the human eco system in the space of 50 years.

All the more reason, then, as we go forward, to set the stage for getting it right in the 21st century. As discussed in the earlier chapters of this book, the consequences of making the wrong decisions have become too costly, too damaging for Planet Earth, to allow them to continue. Growing populations and squeezed resources indicate that the "window of opportunity" for surviving and sustaining disasters has shrunk.

The problems we will have to grapple with — and make decisions about — in the 21st century are already raising their heads: issues of disease and health, including new epidemics; issues of food and feeding the population; issues of environmental protection and climate change, which affect health and the food supply; issues of damaged people, with the damage stemming from war, dislocation and, in many currently wealthy countries, factors such as a sabotaged education system.

For although war and famine may seem to be far more serious threats, one of the greatest threats any group of people, such as a nation, faces, in an Information Age or a Knowledge Economy, is the vast number of damaged young people, damaged by declining standards in the education system.

Already by the late 20th century, a university degree had displaced a high school diploma as being the bare minimum necessary to gain a foot-hold in the workplace. The level of skills in literacy and numeracy once only needed by the top 15% of the workforce are now essential at the very lowest levels. But a great many high school graduates are deficient in these areas now and cannot find sustainable employment — what lies ahead as even the most basic of jobs requires the skills which only a small fraction of university graduates will possess?

At a time when human brain power is the "capital" we have to work with, we are facing several decades of poorer quality brain capital as young people enter the workforce — if they can even find jobs — and participate in businesses. And participating in business means participating in decision making. Which is why assessing and measuring what individuals bring to the table by way of analytical and thinking skills will become even more crucial as the premium placed on the role of information increases.

Earlier in this book, we talked about education systems and the advantage of nations; a corollary of this is the potential of a Brain Drain. Although this is not a new phenomenon, particularly not in the developed world which has long attracted the best and brightest from the developing world, as the role of brain capital intensifies and information content becomes even more mission critical, nations which can still attract the best brains will be the winners. But will those nations still be those of the developed world? At a time when many western nations have debased their educational coin, making them even more dependent on imports of brain capital, increasing opportunities in the developing world may make migration less attractive and may even reverse the historical precedent, as the best and brightest from the developed world leave for those countries on the ascendancy.

The new century will indeed, bear no resemblance to the one coming to a close. As information content becomes more and more pivotal to the businesses of the 21st century, its use in decision making will become more critical, as will the abilities of those making the decisions. For then as for now, in all manner of decision making, excellence begins in the mind.

Selected References

"Intelligent Room," *MIT Research Digest*, April 1998, p. [1].
"Seinfeld-in-Spanish Possible Thanks to SFU Software" *Simon Fraser University News*, July 14, 1998 (press release).

Acknowledgments

Leonard Fuld — Fuld & Co., The Fuld & Company Building 126 Charles Street, Suite 2, Cambridge, MA 02141-2130, Phone: 617/492-5900, Fax: 617/492-7108, E-mail: Info@fuld.com. Web: http://fuld.com
Leonard Fuld is President of Fuld & Co., a leading competitive intelligence consulting firm headquartered in Cambridge, MA. The firm provides detailed strategic and tactical information about public or private firms as well as in-depth market industry studies (U.S. and abroad). Fuld & Co. also presents public seminars and consults on the design of ongoing intelligence programs. Mr. Fuld is the author of many articles and books about competitor intelligence Competitor Ingelligence (Wiley, 1985); Monitoring the Competition (Wiley, 1988); and The New Competitor Intelligence (Wiley, 1995).

Myles P. Kelly — The Marketing Audit, Inc., 1524 Pine Street, Philadelphia, PA 19102, Phone: 215/545-6620, Fax: 215/545-0888, E-mail: mkelly@world-lynx.net
Myles P. Kelly is President of The Marketing Audit, Inc., a leading global consulting firm headquartered in Philadelphia, PA. The Marketing Audit has been providing marketing research, business intelligence, market assessment, industry benchmarking, and customer satisfaction measurement on a custom project basis for reknowned clients in a variety of industries since 1984. Mr. Kelly has conducted symposiums for the Society of Competitive Intelligence Professionals (SCIP), the Association for Global Strategic Information (AGSI), Society of Insurance Research (SIR), the Life Insurance Market Researchers Association (LIMRA), the Drug Information Association (DIA) and The Cambridge Institute. He is the author of numerous articles, including "Assessing the Value of Competitive Intelligence" in *The Journal of AGSI*,

November, 1993, and co-author of "Hot-Air Ballooning in Intelligence Land," in *The Journal of AGSI*, March, 1996.

Seena Sharp — Sharp Information Research, 1122 10th Street, Hermosa Beach, CA 90254, Phone: 310/379-5179, Fax 310/379-1030, E-mail: ssharp@sharpinfo.com

Sharp Information Research was established in 1979 and today provides strategic marketing intelligence for new market entry, line expansion, and business development. The company delivers future-focused perspective and macro view - to discover opportunities, threats, market shifts and substitute competitors. Projects include in-depth research and analysis. Ms. Sharp is a frequent contributor to publications on the subject of market intelligence and also regularly speaks at conferences and seminars.

Index